Managing the International Company: Building a Global Perspective

by

Ronald E. Berenbeim
Senior Research Associate

A Research Report from The Conference Board

Table of Contents

Tables

Exhibits

Charts

AUTHOR'S ACKNOWLEDGMENTS

The author wishes to thank the Conference Board staff colleagues who were involved in various stages of the project. Richard A. O. Brown, then of The Conference Board in Europe, assisted in the preparation of the survey questionnaire. Mary Mauksch of the European office arranged interviews with key European executives. Jeremy Bacon was helpful on issues pertinent to the board of directors. James Basche and Allen Janger offered suggestions on European companies and the appropriate individuals to contact for interviews. Earl Bailey, Ruth Shaeffer, and Virginia Yorio participated in the development of the survey questionnaire. Harold Stieglitz and Lillian W. Kay provided more than the usual amount of editorial support, and James Greene made many helpful suggestions in the area of international business practices.

Highlights

IF THERE is one prospect for the 1980's on which top executives of many large U.S. and European companies agree, it is the anticipation of major growth for their organizations outside their own countries. Over three-quarters of the U.S. participants in this study expect substantial activity within the next decade in at least one region outside their own country. European expectations of growth in foreign environments are even more pronounced; over 90 percent of the European companies predict important activity outside of Europe within the next decade.

The current level of international business and the outlook for the future have had the effect of involving foreigners in top management positions in large U.S. and European companies. To date, this effect is most pronounced at the local level, where 80 percent of the American and 70 percent of the European companies surveyed currently employ a local national at the head of a majority of their countrywide operations abroad. Comments from many of these companies emphasize the relative autonomy of these local units and the local manager's discretion to make important day-to-day decisions. For this reason, the report includes company policy and current practice with respect to local managers in its discussion of top management of international companies.

At the corporate level, the participation of foreigners is less pervasive. Nonetheless, 60 percent of the U.S. and European participants have introduced a foreign perspective through one of three means: (1) a foreign director, (2) a foreign top executive, or (3) a foreign advisory board.

In addition, both American and European companies have endeavored to broaden the horizons of their own nationals through foreign assignments, group planning sessions, audit procedures, informal meetings, and publications. This study also reveals the continuing sensitivity of companies to the need on the part of the local manager for facility in the local language, regardless of the nationality of the individual who has been given the assignment. The survey data show that companies from non-English speaking countries emphasize the importance of that language for all local managers.

Source of the Data

The sample was drawn from a list of 300 U.S.-based corporations with significant operations overseas. (Generally this involved organizations with operations in five or more countries and worldwide sales in 1980 of over $500 million.) This list included representative manufacturers, banks, construction, commercial and other service companies. In addition, similar information was sought from 300 European companies with comparable international activity.

These firms do both a substantial volume and percentage of their business in foreign countries. The 85 American survey participants had a median sales figure in 1980 of $2.7 billion, 30 percent of which was in foreign countries. The medians for the 44 European collaborators were $1 billion and 65 percent, respectively. In addition, the median U.S. and European company had a factory, subsidiary, divisional or regional office in 20 countries. In the case of U.S. companies, the median number of countries in which the firm did business was 72; for the European organization this figure was 60.

Survey data were supplemented by interviews with top executives from all over the world with special emphasis on the United States, Europe and Latin America.

Why This Report

In a world that is getting ever smaller, it is getting more difficult to pin down what is meant by an "international" company. Substituting terms like multinational, transnational or even world company does not make it any easier.

Is there something more to being perceived—and operating—as an international company than just doing business in some foreign countries? If so, what?

It strikes us that these are neither semantic nor academic issues. Trying to develop effective global business strategy in a world increasingly conscious of national sovereignty gives special significance to those simple questions. More companies are—and will be—looking to foreign operations for future growth and profits. And "doing business" on an international scale now has new dimensions.

Hence this study. We sought to define an "international" company in terms of criteria that companies with long and substantial experience in foreign operations recognize. And, more significantly, we attempted to identify managerial resources and practices that companies use to enhance both the external and internal appreciation of their increased internationalism. We asked many companies substantially involved in international business: "What is an international company?"; "How do you achieve an international perspective?"

For the composite answers, and their implications for successful international performance, we owe thanks to all the executives in U.S. and European companies who shared their experience and views with us.

JAMES T. MILLS
President

Chapter 1
The International Company—Characteristics and Challenges

THE HAZARD of parochialism is increasing immeasurably in a competitive world of international dimensions. Recognizing this danger, companies, both small and large, are increasingly characterizing themselves as "international" not only in an operational sense, but in the nature of their ken—in their sensitivity to global issues and to local conditions in disparate geographical and cultural regions.

The reasons for this effort at cosmopolitanism are not difficult to fathom. Increasingly, doing business means doing business internationally. Companies that have been involved in foreign markets are now manufacturing and, in some cases, are engaged in research and development in these foreign environments. Although most European companies of any size have been active outside their home market from the beginning, U.S. companies, as a rule, have concentrated on domestic growth.

In recent years the pace of foreign activity for American companies has increased. In addition, while European firms are accustomed to operating outside the domestic arena in *other* European countries, many are now looking outside Europe for future growth. Conference Board survey data indicate that both U.S. and European companies expect this development to continue in the next ten years. When asked where they anticipated significant growth in the next ten years, Europe was named by fewer European companies than the Middle East, Latin America, Asia and the United States. Although the U.S. market was considered promising in this regard by the largest number of American companies, Latin America and Asia received nearly as many responses (Table 1). Indeed, over three-quarters of the American respondents expect major growth in at least one region outside the United States; roughly 60 percent expect it in two regions; and one-quarter in three areas outside the United States. Expectations by European companies of major growth outside Europe are even more pronounced: 90 percent think major growth will occur in at least one continent outside Europe; nearly 60

percent expect important increases in at least two continents other than Europe; and 40 percent think it will occur on three continents.

Even those U.S. companies whose attention remains focused on their home market are finding that it has become an arena for international competition. No business, however local in its outlook or concerns, is immune to the need for an understanding of international conditions. The Midwestern grain farmer, for example, knows that his prospects depend as much on the weather in the Ukraine as they do on the rainfall in Iowa or Minnesota.

In addition, those companies that do operate in foreign countries want and need to be good citizens of the countries in which they are active. This desire has always made good business sense but, increasingly, it has been demanded of these organizations by the imperatives of the times. The breakup of the old colonial empires and the emergence of countries with a strong national identity and pride, where once there was only a colonial administrator, cannot be ignored. A good many companies

Table 1: Regions Where Companies Expect Major Growth in the Next 10 Years

Region of Anticipated Growth[1]	Nationality of Company		
	United States	Europe	Total
Total Number of Companies..........	85	44	129
Europe	20	14	34
Middle East	17	15	32
Africa	17	9	26
Asia...................	37	19	56
Latin America	42	16	58
United States..........	47	28	75

[1]Companies may anticipate growth in more than one region.

have had the need for sensitivity to foreign environments thrust upon them, whereas in the past going into the country merely entailed dealing with the problems inherent in any expansion of business activity.

Judging from the experiences of the 129 large American and European companies with international interests that participated in this study, both the perception and the reality of being an "international company" are changing. The awareness of a need for understanding local conditions around the world and how they fit into the company's global activity is growing. Increasingly, the understanding of this need is translated into efforts to obtain the added insight of foreigners at all levels within the organization—the board of directors, top management, and local operations. In addition, there is tacit evidence that this approach is part of an endeavor to foster an image of the organization as a truly international institution among company employees.

What is the International Company?

There is no definition of an international company that commands widespread agreement. Despite this failure to agree on terms, the status of an individual corporation is seldom in doubt. Indeed, it could be said by those concerned with such issues that although they cannot state with conviction what an international company *is,* they certainly know one when they see it. In fact, when asked to name those companies that they believe to be truly international, and to give reasons for their answers, U.S. and European executives cite relatively few companies, and just three organizations are mentioned repeatedly by both Americans and Europeans—IBM, Shell and Unilever. As to the reasons, one respondent summed up the general mood: "Reasons are obvious."

Yet the reasons are not all that obvious; it is just the identity of individual companies which is obvious—and not the criteria. If, for example, the test of an international company is the volume of sales in foreign countries, virtually every major Belgian, Dutch and Swiss firm would be international because of the relatively small size of their home markets. Alternatively, the oil industry is, almost by definition, international and Royal Dutch Shell is one of the three organizations most widely perceived by American and European executives to be international. Yet for the sheer size and scale of its operations outside its home country, Exxon rivals Shell, although it was chosen as an example of an international company by significantly fewer respondents; Mobil and Texaco were hardly mentioned at all.

History undoubtedly plays a part in the image of a company as international, but it is certainly not decisive. Two of the three most popular choices—Shell and Unilever—trace their origins back to two separate

countries, but IBM, which was mentioned more often than either Unilever or Shell, is strictly American in its ancestry.

These views suggest that internationalism is not always a quality that can be determined by rational calculation. It relates as much to a company's image of itself as a cosmopolitan international institution, and as a respected local citizen in many different countries, as it does to hard and fast rules with respect to volume of business and organizational structure. Still, there are some basic characteristics which, although not conclusive on the subject, do emerge from discussions as important threshold considerations:

(1) *A substantial portion of the company's markets are in foreign countries.* Within this criterion, there are a number of categories which should be distinguished at the outset. As will be observed by reviewing these distinctions, there are circumstances among companies that do a substantial amount of international business that can greatly complicate the effort to develop an international approach.

The first distinguishing characteristic is the *amount* of international business. With their large home markets, even the most internationally active American companies are more likely to have a smaller percentage of foreign business than their European counterparts. Even among their European counterparts, British, French and German companies are almost certain to have a larger home market than are Belgian, Dutch or Swiss firms. Thus an American company that does 30 percent of its business in a foreign country may be more "international" within the context of this discussion than a Belgian company that accounts for 50 percent of its trade outside national boundaries.

Second, it is important to examine the *nature* of a company's foreign markets in some detail. The company may do a substantial amount of business in one or two geographically and culturally contiguous markets. A U.S. company that does a lot of business in Canada, or a Dutch company with substantial activity in Belgium and Germany, is not faced with problems as formidable as either would be in Japan.

Geography is not the only test. Due to cultural similarities, a British company is likely to have an easier time doing business in such physically distant places as Canada and Australia than in Greece, which is much closer physically to the United Kingdom but has very different cultural traditions.

Moreover the test is not limited to culture and geography. Most South American countries are as far from the United States and as culturally distinct as Europe, but many U.S. companies have a long history of business activity in the former and not in the latter. Even if the particular company in question does not have this history, it has the large body of experience of other companies on which to draw.

When these different categories have been distinguished, it is clear that the most demanding task in developing an international perspective exists where the company is attempting to gain a foothold in a geographically and culturally distant country in which neither it, nor most of the other companies in its own country, has a significant record of participation. There are at this time many companies in both the United States and Europe that find themselves in just such a position and it is likely that their number will increase.

(2) *The company is engaged in a variety of business activities within the host country.* While many companies that have purchasing or sales offices in foreign countries undoubtedly regard themselves as international, it is unlikely that they are involved with the range of local concerns that a company must have if it both manufactures and distributes in a foreign environment. This task has been further complicated in recent years by the addition, in many instances, of local research and/or development facilities which support these manufacturing efforts independent of corporate involvement.

In this regard, the most international companies are engaged in a roughly comparable range of activities in connection with the production and distribution of certain goods in foreign countries as they employ for those products in the home country. Finally, whatever the company's management philosophy may be with respect to issues such as centralization and decentralization, there is generally an effort among the most international organizations to manage the firm's foreign activities with the same degree of coherence and control as is exerted with respect to various branches of domestic operations.

(3) *The company's activities in a foreign environment are of a sufficient magnitude and scope that it must be responsive to the same local constituencies and governmental pressures as a domestic corporation in that country.* Thus, for example, a subsidiary of a U.S. food or drug company operating in Brazil will have the same problems with respect to government regulation, labor supply, wage demands, and consumer criticism as a Brazilian company of comparable size and active in the same industry would have. In light of this fact, a comprehensive understanding of local conditions and personal contact with local elites is not just helpful, it is essential.

(4) *A company's effort to become an international organization is likely to be reflected in its choice of individuals for positions throughout the organization—the board of directors, top management, and managers of* *local operations.* An important element of a company's search for international perspectives and a more sensitive appreciation of the foreign environments in which it operates is its choice of individuals for key positions.

At this time, a significant minority of U.S. and European firms contacted for this study (roughly one-third of the American and over 40 percent of the European) have a foreigner on the board of directors. Companies that do have a foreigner at this level are more likely than companies that do not to engage in activities and to employ individuals at other levels that reflect a search for international viewpoints, and a self-image as an international institution. Such organizations are more likely to hold board meetings in foreign countries; to have a foreigner in top management; to have at least one foreigner heading a foreign component; to think that a foreigner on the board of directors contributes to their ability to do business in foreign countries; and to expect significantly greater growth in foreign than in domestic markets within the next ten years.

While there is some disagreement as to the value of a foreigner at the board level, roughly 80 percent of the U.S. and European participants think that it is important to employ foreigners, particularly local nationals, at the local level—and over 80 percent have, or are now doing so.

(5) *Notwithstanding these criteria, the large international companies are widely perceived to have a strong identification with their native countries.* There are relatively few international companies that are not anchored to a single national identity. The major exception among large companies is the Anglo-Dutch corporation, which has an equally well-established dual image. This identity is legal, political and economic; it means that the parent company's primary concern is the accommodation of one or two national governments and not the successful amelioration of demands by international organizations such as the United Nations or the European Economic Community. (Of course, subsidiaries must respond to the concerns of *their* host governments.) Although many of these companies would (and some have in interviews) vigorously deny that they are national institutions, the structure of the parent is designed to complement and achieve accord with those political entities to which it must be *most* responsive. In the largest number of cases this entity is a single national government.

Indeed, when asked how they relate to such international nonbusiness organizations as the United Nations and the European Economic Community, most companies replied that they do so primarily through their national governments, and, in some cases—particularly chemical companies—through industry trade associations. The third channel, direct contact between the company and the international body, is quite rare. (See Exhibit 1.)

The large businesses that conform to these general characteristics are concentrated in a surprisingly small number of industries: nonelectrical machinery, electrical and electronic equipment, chemicals (primarily pharmaceuticals), and instruments. In addition, the food and oil industries, while not heavily represented as to the *number* of companies, comprise an unusually large percentage of the biggest companies engaged in international activity.

Besides the need for expanding markets, which is especially great in a few key industries, other factors play a role in the development of a company as an international organization. One of these is the merger of companies of different nationalities. The most common and successful of these mergers across national boundaries is the Anglo-Dutch corporation. The effective mergers of British and Dutch firms are well known. When asked to comment on why this particular collaboration had been so successful over the years, one prominent British executive said: "I just guess the British and Dutch get on, that's all."

A variant of this approach is the joint venture between firms of different nationalities. Typically it will begin with a specific objective and ripen into a permanent relationship once the partners become aware of ways in which their strengths are complementary. As the degree of joint activity increases, the two companies will act as one organization, but will remain two separate legal entities.

The markets of an international company are also often the product of historical circumstances. For this reason, continental companies usually initiate foreign operations in other European countries; British companies until recently began their foreign activity with Commonwealth countries; and many U.S. companies first entered foreign markets in Canada. Thus, depending on its original nationality, each company may have a primary and secondary international market; that is, two environments, both foreign, but one of which is more familiar than the second due to cultural or geographic ties.

Notwithstanding these various historical circumstances, the primary objective of expansion of activity to a foreign country is the same as increased domestic activity: to enlarge the company's markets and scope of operation and, in the process, achieve higher sales and profits. Undoubtedly, the imperative of moving into foreign markets is clear to a Belgian company at the outset, whereas it may never be required of an American firm at all, but when a U.S. or Belgian organization finally makes this move, the motives are surprisingly similar.

Becoming an International Company

To negotiate the transition from being exclusively or primarily domestic to being international, today's company usually recognizes three imperatives: First, to acquire a global outlook. Whereas in the past its focus was on the economic, political and cultural developments in a single country, it must now incorporate a worldwide view in its range of concerns.

Second, to develop sensitivity to long-range historical and cultural trends in the individual countries in which it wants to do business. In addition to this awareness, it is necessary to nurture the kind of local contacts that will further an understanding of how business is done, help to gain acceptance of the company as a local citizen, and provide the kind of intelligence which makes it possible to anticipate and to cope with changes in local circumstances.

Finally, to foster an image of itself among its employees as a worldwide organization.

European companies, particularly those that originated in small countries, argue that they have had an advantage over their American counterparts because they were organized according to these principles from the beginning. A top executive of a large Swiss company put it this way: "From the very beginning we knew that we were going to have to be an international company. Switzerland has a very small market."

There can be hazards for companies making a transition from a predominantly domestic to an international concern. A global outlook and self image and sensitivity to local issues are valuable as long as they do not interfere with the ability to manage the company as a single enterprise.

Simply put, the problem is one of *integration* and *coherence*. With the increasing intricacy of many operations in foreign countries, and with many different kinds of operations within a given country, local managements have to find a way to *speak with one voice* within that country. In short, many companies are finding it necessary to resolve the kind of organizational problems *within* a foreign environment that, in the past, have existed only on a corporate level. The local operation in a given country needs adequate authority to speak for the company in its representation to the public, the political leadership, and the suppliers and customers within the country. In addition, the company must coordinate its local objectives with a worldwide strategy, organization, objectives and design.

Depending on the circumstances, the problem of integration and coherence can be reflected in more specific concerns. For most large international companies these imperatives require careful consideration as to whether they will organize along product lines or as geographical

Exhibit 1: ICI: Relationships with National Government, Industry Federations, and Intergovernmental Organizations

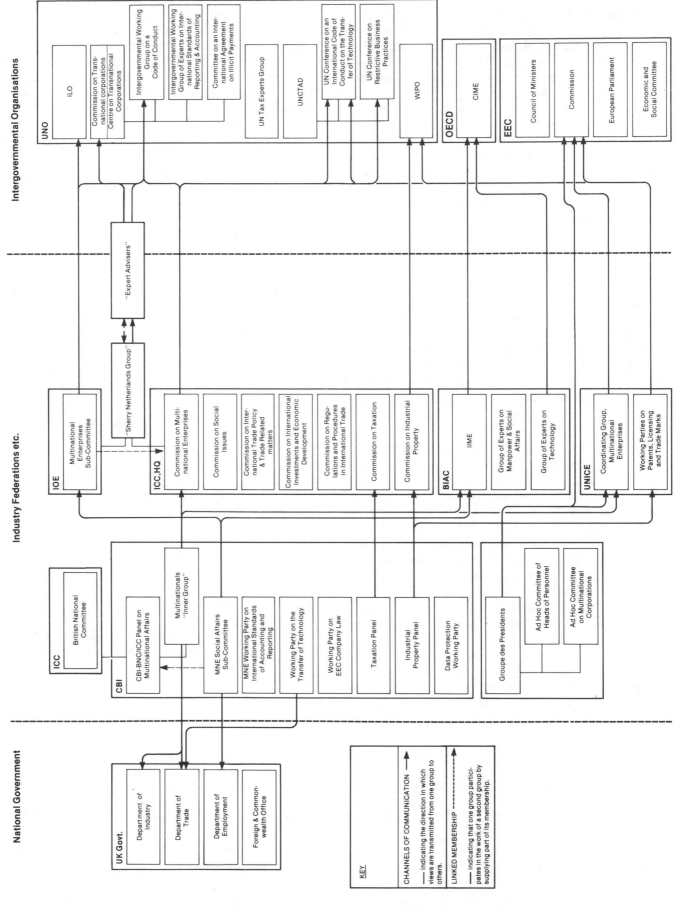

units. European companies are especially concerned with the ultimate effects of codetermination, especially if the laws ultimately vest majority ownership in the workers. One Dutch executive expressed the view of many: "Will there be a conflict of values between national demands, particularly those of labor, and the demands of countries in which you want to do business?"

A similar and more recent problem to confront the international company, particularly in the opinion of Europeans, is the potential effect of the United Nations' proposed code of conduct for multinational businesses. The view with respect to codes—whether mandated by law, as in the case of the U.S. Foreign Corrupt Practices Act, or international pressure through the proposed U.N. code, or implemented by the company—is particularly instructive with respect to the underlying concern of speaking with one voice[1] For some, selecting the right local management is more important than subjecting the local representative to any hard and fast rules. As a Brazilian executive noted emphatically: "What you need is good local management. For myself, I do not need a code to tell me what an act of corruption is." While most agree with this assessment, some feel that the existence of a code can still be helpful in providing guidance to both the company and local managers. As a Canadian executive pointed out: "It is helpful to local management. It is not enough to say, our policy is to obey the law, and pay our taxes, period."

Indeed, codes can provide guidance to local personnel, who may find it difficult to choose between expediency and principle when bribery is heavily embedded in local custom and practice. The existence of a code can bind both the company and its competitors to the more principled course.

An American executive recalled a particular example of how the environment engendered by codes of conduct made it easier to respond to a recent situation: "We were informed by a police chief in an African country that he would expedite the release of furniture from customs for one of our people stationed there for a 'service charge' of $30,000. We told him no."

Codes can help the company to speak with one voice but, in the end, only the manner in which the company is organized can achieve the crucial objective of coherence. A Swedish executive, who is the president of a Swedish subsidiary of a large European firm, put it this way:

"You need a small intelligent headquarters, which leaves these problems to small local autonomous organizations. The worst thing is to have a big and stupid headquarters, but a big and intelligent headquarters can also cause problems." The president of a large American organization added: "Of course, the product will influence how you do it, but what we want is a small local headquarters that speaks with one voice inside the country." This remark shows that both corporate and local executives share a concern as to the importance of coherence. But the American went on to emphasize integration as well: "The parent corporation must be able to monitor these local activities, particularly in the financial area."

Responding to Local Demands

Integration and coherence, though simply stated, is seldom easy to achieve. And it is becoming less easy. For corporate management of a large international company is confronted with a welter of local demands often prejudicial to the "rational" integration and coherence sought. Thus far the demands that are most troublesome come from three major areas: (1) full or partial ownership of the local operation;[2] (2) employment of local managers in important operational positions; and (3) local research and/or development facilities that support local manufacturing and marketing activities and are independent of corporate involvement and interference.[3]

These demands, often couched in the vocabulary of the emergent nationalism and self-respect of the nation state, are advanced by a variety of methods. The most obvious of these is legislation, but the promulgation of new laws is only one aspect of the problem. In many countries bureaucracies command the points of entry for foreign firms and can secure significant concessions through the interpretation of existing laws.

These claims are viewed by corporate headquarters as serious encroachments on their ability to manage. Although local autonomy for both domestic and foreign operations is widely perceived by headquarters to be a

[1]For further discussion of this point, see Joseph LaPalombara and Stephen Blank, *Multinational Corporations and Developing Countries*. The Conference Board, Report No. 767, 1979; Robert Black, Stephen Blank and Elizabeth C. Hanson, *Multinationals in Contention*. The Conference Board, Report No. 749, 1978; and James Greene, *The Search for Common Ground: A Survey of Efforts to Develop Codes of Behavior in International Investment*. The Conference Board, Report No. 531, 1971.

[2]Earlier Conference Board materials that discuss this issue are Robert Black, Stephen Blank and Elizabeth C. Hanson, 1978.

[3]The Conference Board has examined the R&D issue in James R. Basche, Jr. and Michael G. Duerr, *International Transfer of Technology: A Worldwide Survey of Chief Executives*. The Conference Board, Report No. 671, 1975; and Michael G. Duerr, *R&D in the Multinational Company*. The Conference Board, Managing International Business, No. 8, 1970; and Daniel Creamer (with the assistance of Anthony D. Apostlides and Selina L. Wang), *Overseas Research and Development by United States Multinationals, 1966-1975: Estimates of Expenditures and a Statistical Profile*. The Conference Board, Report No. 685, 1976.

good thing, three areas—finance, personnel and research—are generally reserved for corporate direction. Local ownership and control of management and research greatly complicates the task of centralized finance, personnel and research administration.

The Challenge of Local Ownership

Control of local operations through ownership in the foreign business operation is no longer possible to the extent that it once was. Many host countries are now requiring that a substantial amount of the equity participation in a given enterprise be local. The president of a large U.S. company observed: "We used to do business in foreign countries through a division of the parent. Now, due to requirements for local participation, we have to establish subsidiaries and joint ventures." European executives agree that this has also been true in their experience.

In addition, local ownership can lead to local involvement in decision making in other areas which have generally been subject to corporate approval such as divestiture, investment, plant location, and key staffing selections.

Corporate executives see this development as creating problems for them in a number of areas. First, and most important, it affects the control and release of financial data, an activity in which the need for corporate uniformity is particularly great. Local ownership can lead to demands for different treatment of earnings and for the release or withholding of financial data to local shareholders. When these local requirements or shareholder demands vary greatly from one another and from those of the country in which the parent is located, a company's centralized financial administration and its relationship to its own shareholders are threatened.

Not surprisingly, Latin American executives have observed that this trend can ultimately benefit a European or U.S. company. A Venezuelan put it this way: "I have seen many organizations fight tooth and nail to avoid local partners, but the right kind of partner can help. One obvious way they can be useful is with government contacts which are essential in Latin America."

A Brazilian executive noted that the *degree* of company ownership is less important than its relations with its local partners and the use that it makes of them: "I sit on a variety of boards. Because of the shortage of capital in Brazil, not all of them have local financial participation. Some of them are 100 percent company owned; some are mixed; and some are locally owned. The key to effectiveness is how the parent corporation runs the local company. There should be an active and involved local board of directors. Wherever possible, local managers should be hired. This way the company's image as a foreign firm is reduced and people think of it as Brazilian."

Indeed, local financial participation can provide the necessary margin of safety in potentially volatile and sensitive situations—such as the demand for expropriation. As this individual concluded: "In the old days I worried about expropriation. Now, as an affiliate, I worry about the expropriation of the parent by the government of its country."

The Challenge of Local Management

A logical outgrowth of the demand for local participation in the ownership of an international company's local operation is the insistence that the company use local managers. In some instances this demand may come from the local shareholders; in others, from the national government. No company participating in this study could point to an instance where it was required by law.

In fact, countries usually employ indirect methods to achieve this objective. Only one country, India, was cited by more than one company as having exerted strong pressure in this regard. The usual approach is for a host country to drag its feet, or to refuse altogether to approve a work permit for a foreign national. Nor is this problem limited to the entry of top executives. Companies also reported difficulties in getting skilled laborers into certain foreign countries.

The major concern of most companies is that these developments make centralized personnel management and disposition of key management and technical personnel increasingly difficult. The ability to move people around quickly and easily, and to evaluate them uniformly and equitably, encounters serious obstacles. Moreover, companies do not always feel as free to terminate an ineffective manager who is a well-connected local national. On the other hand, an extremely effective person is not always receptive to an offer of promotion to a job in another country, or to corporate headquarters.

There are also special circumstances which many companies feel require the utilization, albeit in many instances on a temporary basis, of one of their own nationals. A takeover, or the early stages of a new operation, fits into this category. Finally, some companies like to reserve at least one important position for one of their own nationals for a variety of reasons such as observation, liaison and career development.

In spite of these concerns, companies will usually yield to local demands for important management positions. The reasons for this are twofold. In the first place, they are finding it increasingly difficult to get their own nationals to accept foreign assignments, particularly where the spouse may also have a career, or where the individual's children are in school. Companies have also found that local managers *can* be helpful in handling local governments, bureaucracies, customers, suppliers and labor relations. Even where the company has concluded that, on balance, it cannot find a qualified local manager, the person dispatched by headquarters often has as a major responsibility the job of training a local successor.

The Challenge of Technology Transfers

The third area in which local demands threaten centralized administration is research. Increasingly, host countries are insisting on control of the technology used by international companies to augment their activities in those countries. This insistence takes the form of demands that the company develop products and processes for local use. In extreme instances the government may even require, in so many words, that the company establish within the country a foundation for scientific capability where none has existed.

For understandable reasons, some companies view this development with alarm. For many organizations, research remains a highly centralized function. There are many reasons for this, but the most obvious are the need for highly trained personnel and the limited availability of such people. Centralization of research ensures the maximum utilization of the large amount of human and economic resources necessary to achieve positive results. Fragmenting this endeavor in a series of local efforts, where the national scientific capability varies greatly can be costly, inefficient, unproductive, and, in the view of some, amounts to a "giveaway" of technology and skills that the company has spent years to develop.

There are other more specific issues. Companies are concerned about the protection of their patents and trademarks. They also see a threat to the repatriation of local profits. Finally, where the parent company has insisted upon the maintenance of centralized research efforts, some host countries have made it difficult for the corporation to recover the costs of research services provided to its local subsidiaries.

For some businessmen these demands are a poorly concealed effort to obtain participation in, or even control of, local enterprises where the country lacks the capital or human resources to own or manage a local subsidiary. A Brazilian businessman observed this trend in his country: "For us, technology transfers are a major issue because there is a shortage of capital in Brazil. As a result the bureaucrats will say you can retain ownership control, but you must transfer technology."

Despite the general alarm, some companies feel that, under certain circumstances, they can live with this development. A German executive discussed some of the factors involved: "It depends on the product and its ties to home markets. If you need to retain control to avoid conflicts of interest, that's one thing. If, on the other hand, it is a completely self-contained program, it matters less."

Others are even sympathetic. A Canadian's comments were in this vein. "Let's say a company's local operation is manufacturing widgets, and it cannot grow beyond that without technical assistance. I don't think that headquarters should withhold this assistance. The local company should be allowed to grow."

But the issue of technology remains an important one for many; perhaps even more important in the long run than ownership or management. Underscoring this high level of concern, an American said: "We would give up ownership for control over the conditions under which we bring materials or services into a country, and control over the conditions under which we are reimbursed by our subsidiaries; these are the critical issues. In our effort to retain this control, it is important to remember that the company's reputation is an important element of control."

Implications for "Internationalism"

The multiplicity of these local demands and their impact on the hitherto centralized administration of finance, personnel and research, complicate the effort to achieve an internationalism that is consistent with the twin objectives of integration and coherence. Judging from the companies surveyed, organizations rely upon two basic tools to accomplish this task: the sensible deployment of personnel on a global scale at various levels of responsibility; and organization and systems that assure sufficient information so that management can develop direction and control. Discussion of individual problems invariably relate back to how the company uses and organizes its people.

Chapter 2
Using Foreigners at the Policy Level

PEOPLE ARE THE KEY in the search for a more global perspective. But at what level? It is useful to look first at the extent to which foreigners have been introduced into areas of overall corporate decision making regarding objectives and allocation of resources; in short, major policy. For analytical purposes these levels include the board of directors and top, or parent company, management.

Foreigners on the Board of Directors

As far as the board of directors is concerned, most international companies do not find it of symbolic importance. An American made this point with the blunt assertion that: "We do not feel the kind of pressure with foreigners that we have experienced with minorities and women to include them on the board, and I do not think that we ever will."

Indeed, the foreign board member is found in a minority of companies. However, the percentage of U.S. (nearly one-third) and European organizations (more than two-fifths) with at least one such individual is significant. Moreover, nearly two-thirds of the American companies that have a foreign board member think that

having such a person in that position helps the company to do business in foreign countries. Roughly half the European companies in this category held this view. By the same token, only one American or European company in ten that does not have a foreign board member believes that such an individual would be helpful in doing business outside the home country.

Among U.S. companies, the foreign board member appears more often among larger organizations, and companies with a high percentage of foreign sales, as well as those that anticipate significant growth in foreign markets. While the largest European companies were also more likely to have a foreign board member, the size of foreign markets, and anticipated growth in these areas, are not distinguishing factors (Table 2).

How Foreign is Foreign?

At the board level, it appears that certain foreigners are preferable to others. Companies evidently value linguistic and/or cultural compatibility more than a local perspective on a potentially large market. In addition, shared experiences play a role in the selection process.

Table 2: Types of Companies that Have a Foreign Director on the Board of Directors

Type of Company	United States		Europe	
	Total Responses[1]	Number of Companies[2]	Total Responses[1]	Responses[1] Companies[2]
Larger companies: United States—over $6 billion; Europe—over $5 billion annual sales	20	9	7	3
Expect significantly greater growth in foreign markets in next ten years	30	12	24	14
High Percentage of sales in foreign markets United States = over 40 percent; Europe = over 60 percent	18	9	18	7

[1]Number of companies meeting definition.
[2]Number of companies with foreign directors.

Table 3: Nationality of Foreign Directors of U.S. and European Companies

Country of Origin of Foreign Director	Nationality of Company		
	United States	Europe	Total
Companies with at least one foreigner on board .	27	18	45
United States	—	6	6
Canada	11	2	13
Latin America			
Argentina	1		1
Brazil	1		1
Mexico	2		2
Venezuela	1		1
Great Britain	9	5	14
Western Europe			
Austria	1	1	2
Belgium	—	2	2
Denmark	1	—	1
France	3	7	10
Germany	2	6	8
Netherlands	—	2	2
Spain	1	—	1
Sweden	1	2	3
Switzerland	1	2	3
Australia	1	2	3
India	—	1	1
Total Number of Foreign Directors	36	38	74

Witness that four out of five of the foreign directors come from one of three places: Canada, Great Britain, or Western Europe. The remainder are from the United States, Latin America, India and Australia (Table 4).

Few foreign directors come from those areas in which most companies expect major growth. (See Table 3.) Although Great Britain and Western Europe account for nearly two-thirds of the foreign directors on American and European company boards, Europe rated fourth, just ahead of the Middle East, as a potential growth area for the 1980's (Tables 1 and 4). As to particular preferences, U.S. companies tend to choose foreign directors from English-speaking countries; roughly 60 percent are in this category. European firms select directors from other parts of Europe; more than 70 percent met this description.

Directors from countries where growth is expected are much less in demand. While the largest number of European companies named the United States as an area in which they expect major growth, Americans hold only six directorships among these companies. Similarly, Latin America was named by 42 U.S. companies, but there are only five Latin American directors of U.S. companies in this group of respondents. Asia, rated highly on both sides of the Atlantic for its growth potential, has furnished the respondents with only one director.

The qualifications possessed by most directors suggest that companies rely on the same network of connections to recruit both foreign and home-country nationals. Many foreign directors appear to have been selected for the same reasons as their fellow board members: (1) experience, (2) expertise, (3) company tradition, or (4) family business connections.

In fact, the credentials of most foreign directors are virtually indistinguishable from those of other board members.[1] The typical foreign director has served three years and is a lawyer, a banker, or an executive of another international company. For the most part, foreign citizenship does not seem to have been a factor in the person's selection.

Pros and Cons

The majority of companies believe that their organizations are truly international in size and scope of

Table 4: Companies with Foreigners in Top Management

Position	30 U.S. Companies
CEO	0
Vice Chairman	1
President	1
President, Chief Operating Officer	1
Regional or Country President	10
Group, Division or Operating Unit President	6
Executive, Senior or Group Vice President	14
Corporate Vice-President or Vice President	32
Controller, Treasurer	2
Group General Manager	1

Position	11 European Companies
CEO	0
Vice Chairman, Executive Committee	1
Divisional or Country President	2
Member Executive Board or Committee	2
Executive or Senior Vice-President	2
Vice President	3
Managing Director or Director	3
General Manager or Manager	3
Senior Adviser	1

[1]For a more detailed discussion of the criteria for membership selection, see Jeremy Bacon and James K. Brown, *Corporate Directorship Practices: Role, Selection and Legal Status of the Board*. The Conference Board, Report No. 646, 1975.

operations. They think that their directors and top management, regardless of nationality, have extensive experience and understanding of international issues. And they view their systems, procedures and subsidiary boards as the primary source of information on local issues.

One U.S. executive summarized this prevailing sentiment: "Many of our directors have international reputations and familiarity with international conditions because they are officers of major multinational or international trading firms, and they bring to the board many of the same qualities and attitudes that a foreigner would." A German participant echoed this opinion: "Because most German individuals on the board of directors hold board positions in foreign multinational companies, an international perspective of top management's decisions is guaranteed."

Many argue that other mechanisms serve the need for an international outlook and for a specific understanding of local conditions. In fact, some think that these other approaches serve that need better than having foreigners on the board of directors ever could.

The key institution in this regard is the local subsidiary. As one American executive put it: "Most international operating groups have their headquarters overseas (e.g., United Kingdom, Germany, France, Australia), and considerable control and influence are exercised from these locations.

"We believe effectiveness abroad depends on our standing in the local community, which would generally be unaware of—and uninfluenced by—the makeup of the parent company board."

Others feel that the role of developing an understanding of foreign environments, and making these various particularized understandings of local concerns part of a global outlook, belongs to management. As one executive observed: "There has been a well-established practice of rotating key executives through international assignments. Therefore the company has a broad base of bicultural experience. Having one or more foreign directors could also be advantageous but their absence has not presented any significant problems."

Other individuals place reliance on formal and informal communications, which are not materially different from those utilized to achieve understanding of domestic markets, for international operations. An American executive stressed the importance to management of "open communications and involvement in the setting of company goals and objectives and for directional communications—up, down, peer group, and CEO field-sensing sessions." A European also emphasized the importance of communications in relating to the world outside the company: "The international activities of our business require permanent contacts with the international partners. This exchange of information

takes place in various ways—among them special conferences and trade organizations."

One of the reasons why most executives think that the development of international perspectives is a management function is that their boards do not really operate in an executive capacity. A European stated bluntly that his company did not need foreign directors because "the board has few executive functions." And an American said: "The board's decisions are primarily based on economic analysis."

This view is in line with the sentiment that any foreigner chosen for the board would not have anything special in the way of expertise to contribute to the kind of decisions the board makes. As a European executive observed: "Decisions are based on business techniques which are not influenced by considerations of nationality." From a U.S. company came the comment: "Our foreign board member is a Canadian, and on most matters his views are similar to those of the other directors." And those who view foreigners as unlikely to make a unique contribution to board discussions or to results obtained by the company received support from an American who recalled that: "We formerly had a foreigner on the board and this seemed to have little influence on the results obtained overseas."

In this regard, the experience of the European companies is instructive. While the European participants are slightly more likely to have a foreign board member (Table 2), foreign board members are not more prevalent among those European companies with a very high percentage of foreign sales or anticipation of a significant increase in foreign sales within the next decade (Table 3). In contrast, U.S. firms in these two categories are much more likely to have a foreign board member than other U.S. firms. This suggests that European companies, which in most instances have been active outside their national boundaries from the beginning, are less motivated by the immediate concern of obtaining this additional insight in choosing a foreign board member.

Still, there are those who think that there is no substitute for a foreigner. In this regard one American executive saw them as a helpful corrective to his board's tendency to view the whole world as an extension of the domestic scene: "In the absence of foreign members and prior to the start of advisory boards, the international decisions of the board of directors were strongly influenced by domestic practices and experiences which were not always applicable in overseas situations."

Despite the need for this kind of "corrective," which is widely acknowledged, most argue that the right vehicle for obtaining it is at the local operational level. A minority said that views on local conditions should be part of board discussions, particularly where substantial operations were involved. One executive put it this way: "A foreign director can bring a local perspective to

Chart 1

American and European Companies Directors' Meeting in Foreign Countries

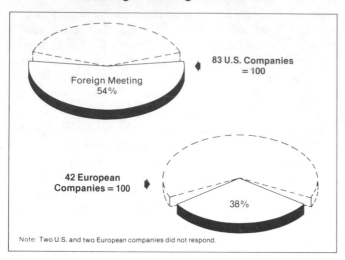

83 U.S. Companies = 100

Foreign Meeting 54%

42 European Companies = 100

38%

Note: Two U.S. and two European companies did not respond.

board deliberations on substantial foreign operations."

Are there particular countries where it is essential to have a national from that country on the board of the parent company if the company wants to do substantial business within that country? Most executives do not think so. Only two countries, France and Japan, were cited with any frequency as places where that could be the case.

As has already been observed, the symbolic importance of the foreign board member is generally discounted, but one executive did state that: "Our image as a multinational gets increased credibility from having foreign board members."

* * *

In sum, there are important areas of agreement between those who see a foreign director as important and those who do not. Most acknowledge the importance of avoiding the pitfall of viewing the international arena as no more than an extension of domestic areas of concern. Those who view foreign directors as unnecessary think that their own nationals are just as capable of achieving this perspective and, perhaps, more likely to understand the company and its problems. For this reason, most of the participating companies would probably agree with the U.S. executive who said: "We have no foreign directors and no reason to believe a foreigner (as such) would make a difference. The *right* foreigner (or American) always will."

Meetings in Foreign Countries

Rather than putting foreigners on their boards, many companies take their boards to foreign shores. Over half

of the U.S. respondents hold directors' meetings in foreign countries. The percentage of European organizations that engage in this practice is lower; slightly more than one-third. All companies characterize such meetings as infrequent or occasional (Chart 1).

The length of these foreign meetings varies, and the meeting is often supplemented by other activities of an educational, social or cultural nature. Because their members travel farther for such an occasion, U.S. companies whose boards convene in foreign countries tend to have longer meetings than do European firms. Despite this longer duration, roughly half the American respondents said that the actual board meeting in foreign countries is about the same length as those held in the United States (Chart 2).

For the most of the U.S. and European companies that have them, the foreign board meeting is an opportunity to have contact with local nationals who are managing key components. Virtually all of the American and European companies said that their foreign meetings included presentations by area managers and tours of local facilities as important elements. For many of these companies, this area manager is a local national; American and European companies who employed at least one foreigner at the head of a local operation were much more likely to have a foreign board meeting.

Some U.S. companies include additional cultural, social and educational events. A spokesman for one company said: "The regular business meeting of the board lasts approximately three hours, as it normally does here. However, there are additional required

Chart 2

Length of Directors' Meeting in Foreign Countries

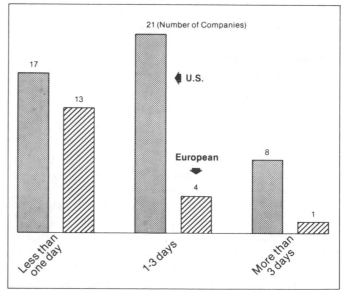

21 (Number of Companies)

17

13

U.S.

European

8

4

1

Less than one day

1-3 days

More than 3 days

sessions dealing with regional history, politics and economics." Another executive described his company's directors' meetings in foreign countries in this way: "The directors' meetings include meetings with political figures, plant visits, presentations by local managers of all nationalities, cultural programs, historical tours, and speeches or performances by national figures in academe or the arts."

The attempt by American companies to familiarize their directors with respect to local conditions in foreign countries is not limited to board of directors meetings. One executive noted: "Our meetings in foreign countries are very infrequent. We do have something of a program for our directors to do some traveling to acquaint themselves with the international operations outside this country. There are certain ground rules for how frequently they can go; I think no more often than one single geographical area every two or three years. They do take fairly extensive trips for which they are reimbursed, and in which they are given well-organized guided tours by the management in that area."

Some individuals question whether these meetings actually achieve the objective of furthering understanding of local conditions, or whether they are even intended for that purpose. One former CEO, who is a director of other companies as well as his own, made this observation about foreign board meetings: "It's a perk, pure and simple. It is hard to attract qualified directors, considering the amount of time it takes and the increased legal responsibilities. This is a little extra. It is a nice trip and you can take your wife along, and tack on a trip of your own at the end."

Survey data provide some support for this assertion. Smaller U.S. and European firms are as likely to hold a foreign meeting as are very large companies. The practice is much less common among middle-sized organizations of all nationalities.

Another former CEO, who is also a director of other large international companies, expressed concern about the expense of these undertakings: "It can be very expensive and there is the problem of security. It is hard enough to provide adequate security for a meeting in the United States. It is much more difficult in a foreign country."

The Foreign Advisory Board

The use of the foreign advisory board as an additional channel of communication to achieve an international orientation is a comparatively recent phenomenon, and most of these boards have been established within the last ten years. (See box.) This practice is not widespread; only one-sixth of the U.S. respondents had such a board, while the percentage for European companies is somewhat higher—just under one in four. Survey data

---

COMPANIES THAT HAVE OR HAVE HAD A FOREIGN ADVISORY BOARD

General Motors
Pan American Airways
R. J. Reynolds
Westinghouse
I.B.M.
Exxon
Chase Manhattan Bank
Sperry Rand
Ford Motor Company
CPC International
Black and Decker
Chemical Bank
Albany International

Sources: Annual Reports; News Releases; Harvard Business Review.

---

suggest that the advisory board is more often a supplement to a relatively high degree of international input through conventional sources than it is a substitute for it. For example, American and European companies that have foreigners on their boards of directors are just as likely to have an advisory board as those that do not. In addition, American and European companies that have a foreigner in top management are more likely to have an advisory board. Companies whose top managers have had extended foreign assignments are also considerably more likely to maintain such an institution.

Company size and percentage of foreign sales is also a factor. Forty percent of the U.S. respondents with annual sales over $6 billion had advisory boards, while the figure for companies with under $6 billion in sales was less than 10 percent. Similarly, over half of the European firms with more than $5 billion in annual sales have an advisory board, while fewer than one company in six of the smaller companies have one.

The picture is the same with respect to the percentage of foreign sales. Among U.S. companies with more than 40 percent in foreign sales, the prevalence is one in three; while for companies under the 40 percent figure, only one in ten have an advisory board. One European company in four with foreign sales over 60 percent has an advisory board, while for those companies with less than 60 percent foreign sales the figure is one in five.

While some commentators have dubbed these mechanisms "international advisory boards," current practice suggests that a more accurate term would be "foreign." The general international advisory body is favored by only one survey participant. For the most

For some European companies language can be a problem not just in Brazil or Indonesia, but also in day-to-day operations and in board of directors' meetings in their home country.

Consider the following case of a Belgian company. Depending on the location of its headquarters in this small country, the local language will be Flemish or French. (In Brussels, French is spoken in some sections and Flemish in others.) Yet the board of directors conducts its business in English, rather than Flemish or French.

In addition to this Belgian corporation, there are two Dutch companies that speak Dutch at company headquarters and English in board of directors meetings. Of four Finnish companies, one conducts board meetings exclusively in Swedish; the other three employ both Swedish and Finnish. Finally, a German company uses English despite the fact that it has no foreign directors.

Europeans, particularly those from small countries like Belgium, Holland and Switzerland are quite matter-of-fact about this state of affairs. In Belgium and Switzerland, they are used to the need for more than one language to do business in their own country. Still, although the need for language facility in foreign countries is widely acknowledged, it evidently is not a significant factor in board of directors' meetings and in the operations of corporate headquarters.

At the board or corporate levels a company would seem to have two choices. It might opt for sensitivity and diversity—having executives who speak many languages and translating corporate communications into several different tongues; or it might attempt to impose some kind of standardization by adopting a single language for board meetings, planning sessions, and correspondence.

For the most part, companies respond to these alternatives by choosing neither exclusively. Rather, a mix of approaches is used.

Although most companies favor the local language for board meetings, English is often the choice for international planning sessions and communications among local subsidiaries.

Most companies do not elect standardization over tradition in the choice of language for a board meeting. If the organization was founded as a Dutch company, it is likely, although far from certain, that the board will speak Dutch when it convenes. The preservation of this tradition, particularly in cases where the language is not widely spoken by people in other countries, is likely to be an important factor in whether or not the company has any foreign directors.

A Swiss company, long accustomed to the need for multilingualism within its own borders, actually attempts to accommodate a number of different languages in its board meetings, which to an American must sound something like a meeting of the United States Security Council without earphones. The former secretary of the corporation described the policy in some detail:

"For board of directors meetings we speak what we call 'High German,' or proper German. Amongst ourselves, when in the executive committee, for instance, we speak dialect. We have an Englishman who has been with us so long that he actually understands the dialect.

"This dialect differs substantially from German, especially in pronunciation. It would be very difficult for a fellow from Frankfurt or from Berlin to understand us when we talk normally. We also have an American, who can speak both the dialect and German because he lived in Switzerland as a student. Once in a while, though, you have someone, let us say the head of a project in England who is making a presentation. He is Australian. He attends the board meetings to report on our activities in England. When this happens, the meeting switches over to English.

"If someone wanted to make a presentation in French, the board would convert to French. I think, though, Italian would be overdoing it a little. If someone spoke Italian slowly, most of the members would probably be able to follow the broad outlines of his report, but only that. High German is commonly the language when the country in question is neither French or English speaking. It so happens that the head of our Italian operation is Italian. We can easily discuss problems with him in English. As he does not speak German, English is really the common denominator."

The charm of this adaptation to cultural diversity gives way to the imperative for standardization in the company's annual two-day planning session where everyone speaks English. Indeed, for many companies English has become the language of communication between the parent and its affiliates. A Dutch executive, whose company continues to hold its board meetings in Dutch, commented on the need for standardization:

"It is now desirable to introduce a standard language with the object of having expert information in one language. Now we expect all qualified people in this company to be able to at least read English, and preferably to express themselves orally in English so that international, you might say multinational, discussions are carried out in English."

This individual recalled that the use of English as an international language became widespread after World War II. Prior to that international dialogue was conducted in the local language or in French:

"In former times, let's say before World War II, I guess the major communications links were bilateral. If you were conducting business with a plant in Poland or in Barcelona, you spoke to them in Polish or Spanish. If there was a second language, it was mainly French. Now you will find that the younger generation have all switched over to English. Earlier, as a manager or as an engineer, you had to know French to get along in a place like Barcelona or in Italy; now you need English."

part, companies that have an advisory body prefer a regional focus, such as Latin America or Europe. In four instances, companies have an advisory board for a single country; there are two such committees for Brazil and one each for Australia and Japan.

U.S. companies that have an advisory board express a high degree of satisfaction with them; 86 percent said that they were helpful in international business activity. Virtually all of those that do not have such a committee (94 percent), however, do not feel that adding one would help.

The European attitude toward advisory boards is much less favorable. Of those that have them, less than one in three think they are helpful. Among those that do not, the figure is less than one in five.

The individuals selected for these councils fall into one of two categories:

(1) *Regional figures who can be helpful in promoting the company's interests and specialists with knowledge of the region or country.* An example of this approach was cited by the company spokesman who said: "Our advisory board includes local businessmen, who are knowledgeable about the local business environment and governmental policies. These individuals must also have sufficient stature to open the way for government contacts and to provide advice on local policy matters."

(2) *Individuals with broad international experience.* An executive from a company that chooses this kind of person states: "We look for senior industrialists, economists, bankers, academicians and former government officials with diverse experience, capable of objective insight, advice and counsel on economic, social and political conditions and trends."

How It Is Used

Companies establish and utilize advisory councils for a variety of objectives. Most advisory boards, however, exist to further one or both of two major aims:

(1) *To serve as an "early warning system."* This kind of advisory committee will be involved in such activities as environmental assessments; advice on the handling of specific local problems, analysis of long-term regional political, cultural and economic trends; and developing the company's sensitivity to local issues.

(2) *To improve the company's business prospects in a particular region or country.* Companies expect this type of advisory board to help them in developing contacts with local governmental officials and potential customers. It is likely that a company with this objective would look to its advisory board for advice on how its products should be adapted to local markets.

Whatever the company's motives may be in establishing an advisory board, observers are agreed on the importance of stating them with clarity and precision at the outset (Exhibit 2). In addition, it is important to familiarize board members with company practices and objectives. Finally, it is helpful to involve high-level corporate officers, such as the CEO, in the committee's activities.

Pros and Cons

As has been stated, those companies that have advisory boards think that they have been helpful. This is especially true where the company expects the board to give *advice,* rather than to develop specific business opportunities. One executive summarized this view: "The advisory board has provided an early warning of trends to which it was imperative we be sensitive, as well as a balanced understanding of the various international issues which have an impact on our business." In spite of the satisfaction among the companies that have them (particularly in the United States), most of the respondents do not feel that the presence or absence of advisory boards has had any effect on their ability to do business in foreign countries.

The view of those who did expect the board to develop business prospects is expressed by a European respondent: "An international or regional advisory board or council should have come up with more business opportunities abroad."

Virtually all of those who think them unnecessary, feel that their role is already being performed by some other group within the company. Commonly cited in this regard are: (1) the board of directors, (2) the board of directors of subsidiaries, (3) functional management, and (4) local management within foreign countries. In general, these companies think that their own directors and employees had the same broad training and experience as any potential advisory board member. And such individuals better understand the needs and limitations of their own companies. Of course, those who do think that this need can be met within the company emphasized the importance of communication, both formal and informal, to insure maximum utilization of important information.

In short, the need for, or value of, an advisory board depends on the use to which it will be put and whether the proposed use is sufficient to justify the expense. For those who are not sure of what the use will be, its necessity is hard to justify. As an executive of a food manufacturer put it: "I am not sure of what the role of an advisory board is. It is OK for bankers, who are not terribly sophisticated in international business; for them it may be helpful. I do not think that it is useful with our divisional organization. We do have special subject advisory boards on issues such as food and nutrition.''

Top Management

Clearly, it is the major corporate officers—the top management—that international companies look to to combine the directors' breadth of understanding as to international developments with a thorough knowledge of the company's own global strategy. It is this top management level that is relied upon for an awareness of specific local developments in vastly different regions of the world, and it is in the corporate office that this information is integrated into the company's overall strategic design. And it is the identity of top management which is viewed as projecting on a daily basis the company's image as a truly international organization both to itself and to the outside world. To the companies participating in this survey, it evidently does not require a heavy influx of foreigners to achieve this perspective or image.

Prevalence of Foreigners

Among U.S. companies slightly more than one-third have a foreigner who is a top manager, while the figure for European companies is roughly one-fourth. For most organizations the presence or absence of a foreigner in a top management position has little relation to the company's ability to operate effectively in foreign markets. Companies that have a foreigner in top management are not more likely to think that such an individual can be helpful in international business activity than are companies that do not have a foreigner within their top ranks.

The larger American companies (over $6 billion in annual sales), however, are more likely to have a foreigner who is a top corporate officer. Size is not a factor among European companies.

In addition, U.S. and European companies with a higher percentage of foreign sales are more likely to have a foreigner in top management. Among American companies that do more than 40 percent of their business in foreign countries, two-thirds have a top manager who is a foreigner; the figure for companies that have under

40 percent of their sales in foreign countries is only 28 percent. Over one-third of the European companies with more than 60 percent of their sales in foreign countries have a top executive who is a foreigner, while only one-eighth of the companies with foreign sales below 60 percent have such an individual in their corporate headquarters.

Still, the U.S. and European companies that do have foreigners who are high-level corporate executives are likely to value internationalism in certain other respects. For example, those American and European companies that have a foreigner in top management are more likely to have other top managers who have had extended foreign assignments. American companies that have a majority of foreign components headed by local nationals are also more likely to have a top executive who is a foreigner.

Who They Are

None of the responding American or European organizations has a CEO who is a foreigner. American companies have more high-ranking individuals and are more likely to have more than one such person than are their European counterparts. To a certain degree this reflects the tendency of U.S. companies to include divisional and regional presidents within their top-management groups. Foreigners active in top management with American companies include one president and chief operating officer; one president; and one vice-chairman. European companies have only one individual at this level—the vice-chairman of the executive committee. Nearly all of the foreigners mentioned as top executives with both American and European companies are general executives; very few are identified as functional or staff executives: there are only two controllers and no heads of legal departments (Table 4).

The higher percentage of American companies employing one or more foreigners in top positions suggests that, despite the large number of countries that are concentrated in Western Europe, political and cultural obstacles to the employment of foreigners remain. A Swiss executive, whose company is only a few miles from both the French and German borders, noted that relatively few people in corporate headquarters lived in and commuted from these countries. In his view, Swiss law was a factor in this regard, but not a controlling one: "Corporatewise we have certain limitations as far as the law is concerned. Working permits for foreigners have become a problem due to the overpopulation of Switzerland by foreigners. But for practical purposes, and in the numbers we are talking about, we have no problems."

An observation by a Dutch executive suggests that the relatively small number of foreign executives in Dutch firms may have more of a cultural than a political or legal explanation: "Our company headquarters is close to the Belgian border and we do a lot of business in Belgium. The Dutch language is not a problem for Flemish Belgians, whose language is virtually the same. For these reasons I often wonder why we have not attracted a Belgian executive. I think it is the French lunch hour, which exists throughout Belgium, and is, of course, more than an hour and involves an elaborate meal at home or in a restaurant. I don't think that the Belgian executive is willing to give that up for a sandwich at his desk."

Why and Why Not

As might be expected, there are substantial similarities and a few differences between the pros and cons of having a foreigner in top management and the rationale for a foreign presence on the board of directors.

Positive comment as to the benefit of having a foreigner in a top management position focused on the need for an additional perspective, rather than any direct business advantage. Although most said that a foreigner in a top position does not help the company to do business in foreign countries, many still think that it is desirable to have a foreigner at a high level within the company. A European executive put it this way: "The world becomes one big shopping center. All influences are needed, the more diversified the better."

Some U.S. companies share this view. An American executive said: "Presence cannot have other than a positive effect," while other companies stressed the "broadened perspective and awareness," and the "better insight into foreign problems and mentality," that a top manager from a foreign country can add. One individual noted some of the problems his company had encountered because of the lack of foreigners at higher levels within the company: "We lack a broad perspective and domestic companies become too U.S.-oriented in their competitive analysis. There is a poor understanding of risks and opportunities in markets other than the United States." Another executive expressed satisfaction with the contribution made by a foreign top manager within his company: "A foreigner as head of international pharmaceuticals has a broad perspective which U.S. nationals do not always have."

While most of these observations are interchangeable with those that could be made about foreigners on the board of directors, one European respondent saw specific ways in which foreigners can be helpful in top management positions: "The presence of foreigners in corporate positions can: (1) increase the flexibility in key management transfers from headquarters to subsidiaries; and (2) ease and make effective communication in both directions between subsidiaries and headquarters."

One company has the unique problem of too many foreigners in top management positions. As an American spokesman for this Saudi Arabian company observed: "A good many of our top managers are non-Saudis. What we need at this point in time is to find more qualified Saudi Arabians."

In all of these responses the omissions also tell a story. Very few companies pointed out that a foreigner could help them increase sales or gain access to new markets. By and large, those companies that thought a foreigner in top management could be helpful valued the "perspective" and the "insight" that such an individual could lend to discussions at the highest level. The benefits of this additional point of view were, in the opinion of most respondents, a more significant consideration than any specific operational gains to be achieved.

Among those who think that foreigners in top management do not have a bearing on the company's ability to do business in foreign countries, there is a widely shared view that, as one European put it: "It could have an effect, but it is not an objective in itself." Americans share this view that a foreign executive should meet other criteria in addition to being foreign. An American observed: "We concentrate on finding the right, good people irrespective of national origin (although we try to put them in the right jobs in the right places)." Another American noted that while being foreign could be helpful, possibly other things were more important: "The presence of foreigners in executive management has some benefits; however, personal characteristics other than nationality are more significant."

Another reason why some view foreigners in top management as unnecessary is that the current management had ample foreign experience of its own. An American executive observed that: "As long as the people in corporate are experienced in managing overseas operations and/or are sensitive to the peculiarities of managing overseas operations, there is no particular loss by having no foreigners in corporate positions."[2]

[2]Many individuals who are employees or citizens of the foreign countries where American firms maintain operations do not share this view. They argue that the length of foreign assignments is much shorter for American companies than it is for their European counterparts and that as a result, American executives do not leave the country with an adequate understanding of local needs. In addition, local nationals who are managing local operations of American corporations complain of rigid centralization and a lack of corporate sensitivity to their problems. This insensitivity, in their opinion, is due to the lack of experience of corporate managers with conditions outside their own country. See Joseph LaPalombara and Stephen Blank, *Multinational Corporations in Comparative Perspective.* The Conference Board, Report No. 725, 1977; and Joseph LaPalombara and Stephen Blank, *Multinational Corporations and Developing Countries.* The Conference Board, Report No. 767, 1979.

Many American and European executives think that developing international perspectives and an understanding of local problems in foreign regions is the responsibility of some element other than top management. Although a few organizations mentioned the board of directors or advisory committees in this regard, most consider this to be the role of the company's various local operations in foreign countries. Supporting this view one executive said: "As long as management within the respective foreign countries is heavily weighted with local nationals—it is not necessary to have foreigners at the corporate level." Another individual made a similar point with respect to his company's approach to decentralization: "Once established, foreign subsidiaries are, to a large extent, locally autonomous and staffed as soon as is practicable with local managers who are responsive to local business conditions."

Finally, conversations with executives underscore the importance of communications, both formal and informal, between corporate headquarters and local operations. Although the majority of companies consider foreigners at the top of the organization to be unnecessary, there is general agreement that top executives need exposure to local conditions in foreign countries through extended assignments in foreign operations, travel and face-to-face contact with local managers.

The Value of Foreign Assignments

Where companies expect their own nationals to supply the same insight as a foreigner, the usual justification for this view was that many of the organization's top managers have had extensive experience in foreign countries. In this regard a European observed: "Nationality is not important; interests and experiences are—and they can be international irrespective of nationality."

There is ample evidence that this view is widely shared among American and European companies. In both cases, the foreign assignment has become an important element of the ambitious executive's resume. A comment by the chief executive of a large European company suggests that a foreign tour of duty will continue to be an experience that many top executives share: "Increasingly, people are asking 'what will happen when I get back?' In some instances they want assurances of a good job when they return. This makes sense from our point of view, too. Of course, you can only offer a 'return ticket' to your best managers, so those are in most instances the ones that get these assignments."

Whatever the future may hold, the foreign assignment is a common experience among current top executives. Over two-thirds of the U.S. companies and over three-fourths of the European firms reported that at least one of their top managers had worked in a foreign office.

Table 5: Foreign Assignments of American and European Top Management

	Nationality of Parent		
Country of Service	United States	European	Total[1]
United States	—	7	7
Canada	8	4	12
North America		2	2
Western Europe			
General Europe......	21	2	23
Ireland		1	1
Great Britain	11	6	17
Belgium	6		6
France	7	3	10
Germany	1	3	4
Italy	2	4	6
Netherlands	2	2	4
Switzerland.........	1		1
Sweden		1	1
Greece		1	1
Portugal............		1	1
Spain	1	1	2
Latin America			
General Latin			
America............	6	1	7
Caribbean	1		1
Honduras...........	1		1
Brazil	4	2	6
Mexico.............	4		4
Colombia...........		1	1
Venezuela	5		5
Australia	3	4	7
Japan................	5	1	6
Philippines	1		1
Egypt		1	1
Iran.................	2		2
India................	1		1
Pakistan	1		1
Kenya...............	1		1
Far East.............	1	1	2
Pacific	2		2
Africa...............	1	1	2
General International...	3		3
Too many to mention ...	7	2	9
No. of Companies......	85	44	129

[1]Details add to more than total number of companies because of multiple responses.

Among the American firms in this category, the median percentage of top executives with foreign experience was 15 percent, and for the European organizations it was over 25 percent. The median length of a foreign assignment for both U.S. and European executives was between three and four years.

The geographic range of this service includes virtually every region in the world (Table 5). There is evidence that this experience is considered useful in its own right and is not always awarded to acquaint the individual with specific knowledge of a growth market. For example, the number of companies whose executives have experience in Western Europe (77) is far and away the largest of any region, even though the area is regarded as relatively unpromising for growth by both U.S. and European companies. On the other hand, relatively few European top executives (7) have had experience in the United States, the area in which the largest number of European companies expect major growth in the next 10 years.

Finally, it should be noted that the foreign assignment is a little less "foreign" in European companies. Roughly half of the European assignments were to other European countries, and nearly three-quarters of them were to Europe or North America. Americans, by and large, traveled further in terms of culture, geography or both. Half of the Americans served in a European country, and when Canada is added the number rises to 60 percent. The balance, a far larger proportion than in the case of the European group, were assigned to Latin America, Asia, Africa, the Middle East, and Australia.

The reasons for assigning a particular individual to a foreign post are varied, but four broad categories (which are not mutually exclusive in a given case) can generally be discerned: (1) developmental, (2) transfer of technology or business knowledge, (3) unique business needs, and (4) contract fulfillment. (See Exhibit 3.) IBM, the company that provided this statement of its world-wide policy for international positions at all levels, notes that in more cases than not at least two of the criteria are met. The company estimates that development is at least one reason for a quarter of its foreign assignments; technology or knowledge transfers are a factor in over 40 percent of foreign work details; and unique business needs or contract fulfillment are an element in nearly one-third of the assignments.

Whatever an individual company's policy guidelines may be, both American and European executives emphasize the development and knowledge transfer aspects of the equation. They stress the general value of a foreign tour of duty, the need for adaptation and for making independent decisions. Finally, they see the requirement of training a local successor to be an important experience for their own nationals as well as for the local individual who received the instruction. Many commented that the individual was sent to a particular place at a given time because that was the only opportunity within the company for that person to get a particular kind of experience. No one said in so many words that "we sent Mr. A. to Brazil because we expected that both he and Brazil would be important to our company in 10 years." Rather, the approach was: "At that point in Mr. A's career we wanted him to have the experience of being an area manager. Such a position was available in Brazil."

Exhibit 3: IBM: Reasons for Foreign Assignment

CODE	FUNCTION
1	*Development*—The purpose here is to develop and strengthen the skills, sensitivities and viewpoints of individuals. Included with this group will be both those who have been identified as current or probable participants in executive resource systems and those whose assessed capabilities may not carry them to executive levels of the business but who can and should be developed for enhanced contribution in their home country.
2	*Transfer Activity*—Included herein would be transfer of technology, transfer of product, and transfer of knowledge. An example of technology would be a semiconductor manufacturing process; an example of a product would be a customer engineering technical operations group that is assisting in the announcement phase of the products; and the transfer of knowledge would be an individual who has a knowledge of European compensation programs and is assigned to the Corporate Staff to transfer his knowledge to others.
3	*Unique Business Needs*—Included herein would be situations where experienced local employees are not available—e.g., developing countries or application development centers where first-hand knowledge and experience is required in the use of an application. Situations in which we have not as yet developed local competence, although resources are in training or otherwise contemplated, would also fit the business need definition.
4	*Contract Fulfillment*—Those who are assigned to carry out military and/or governmental contracts. Cost is borne by the contracting agency. (This category is applicable to the U.S. only.)

The above are not mutually exclusive and, in more cases than not, at least two of the criteria will be met.

We wanted him to have the experience of being completely in charge of a local operation and serving as a company spokesman. We wanted to see how he could function in a foreign environment, and we wanted to see how effective he could be in training a successor and developing a strong local staff. This job seemed ideal from that point of view.''

The Americans and Europeans who have worked in foreign offices have had almost every kind of job imaginable—from geologist and area chemist to president of the company's European operations. Currently they are all top executives in the corporate offices of their companies. Among the Americans this includes six CEO's, two chairmen, one vice-chairman, one president and chief operating officer, and seven company presidents. The European list of corporate foreign service alumni contains the names of one chairman and three company presidents.

Naturalized Citizens

In addition to foreigners and nationals with substantial foreign experience, companies can rely on foreign-born naturalized citizens for added insight in doing business in foreign countries. A top executive with an American company, who is foreign-born, observed that such individuals have a significant contribution to make: ''I think that you should not limit your examination to foreigners. Look to see if the company has foreign-born naturalized citizens in important positions. In my case, the fact that I was foreign born has given me greater understanding and empathy for other countries and cultures.''

Survey data demonstrate that U.S. companies often have the benefit of this perspective; 40 percent employ foreign-born naturalized citizens as top executives. This list includes four CEO's, one chairman of the board, one president and chief operating officer, and one chief financial officer. The individuals come from many different countries and regions of the world. Among them are Canada (six), Great Britain (eight), Western Europe (fourteen), Eastern Europe (two), Pakistan (one), India (two), Latin America (two), Turkey (one), Iraq (one), China (one), Algeria (one), and Egypt (two).

The European companies do not benefit from this development and European top management is even less likely to include a foreign-born naturalized citizen than a foreigner who has not changed citizenship. Only five companies have naturalized citizens in top management positions.

The Policy Level—An Added Dimension

Internationalism for a company connotes global vision, sensitivity to local conditions, and an image that it projects both to itself and to others of a truly international institution.

The presence of foreigners on boards, advisory committees, or as part of top management suggests that their inclusion at any of these levels is not required, or even meaningful. Indeed, only three U.S. and three European companies of the 129 large international

Table 6: Companies that Have a Foreigner on the Board of Directors, a Foreign Advisory Board, or a Foreigner in Top Management

| | Nationality of Parent Company | |
| | United States (85 Companies) | Europe (44 Companies) |
Practice		
Have all three.	3	3
Foreigner on board and advisory board only. . . .	5	7
Foreigner on board and foreigner in top management only	13	6
Foreign advisory board and foreigner in top management only	6	3
Have at least one.	50	27

Table 7: Use of Foreigner on Board and in Top Management According to Percentage of Foreign Sales and Expectation of Growth in Foreign Markets

| | Nationality of Parent | | | |
| | United States | | Europe | |
Practice	Over 40 Percent Foreign Sales	Expect Growth in Foreign Markets	Over 60 Percent Foreign Sales	Expect Growth in Foreign Markets
Have foreign board member. . .	50%[a]	40%[a]	39%	42%
Have foreign advisory board.	33[a]	17	26[a]	17
Have foreigner in top management	67[a]	48[a]	37[a]	17

[a]Proportion with foreign board members is greater than for other U.S. and European companies in this survey.

participants have foreigners on their boards and in top management and also maintain a foreign advisory committee. However, when a composite is assembled, a different picture emerges. Roughly 60 percent of both the U.S. and European firms do *at least one* of these three things, and one-third of the American and over 40 percent of the European companies do two of them (Table 6).

By a substantial majority in all three cases, both U.S. and European companies do not think that having a foreign board member, a foreigner in top management, or a foreign advisory board helps them to do business in foreign countries. In fact, some companies that do not think that these measures are helpful in this regard nonetheless have foreign participation in corporate decision making or have established an advisory committee. Clearly, developing international perspectives is not always perceived as furthering specific business objectives.

Rather, among the U.S. companies there seems to be a heightening emphasis on the relationship between greater international awareness and business success in foreign environments. This is evident from the apparent connection in American companies between the utilization of these approaches and the size of the company's foreign markets and its anticipation of future growth. (See Table 7.)

For American companies, therefore, a high percentage of foreign sales, or anticipated growth in foreign markets renders the existence of a foreign board member, a foreigner in top management, or a foreign advisory committee more probable than if this is not the case. These factors are much less likely to be important to European companies. Most European companies are doing a very high percentage of business outside the home country and always have been. As to anticipated growth, only one European company expects the major growth in the next ten years to come from its domestic markets. These elements, which are present in relatively few American companies, are found in most European firms.

Moreover, in interviews, Europeans emphasized their long experience with foreign markets and the view that doing business in foreign countries is almost second nature for them. Americans, who are newer at the game, apparently feel a greater need for this kind of perspective at the corporate level.

Chapter 3
Internationalism Through Local Personnel

COMPANIES RELY on the local manager to project both their sensitivity to local issues and concerns and their commitment to building a national organization within the foreign countries in which they do business.

The identity of the local manager may also suggest a great deal about the organization's image of itself as an international institution. For example, one company that relies primarily on its own nationals, views itself as a firm with a cosmopolitan corps of executives who feel at home in a variety of very different cultures. Moreover, as a result of this approach, many of the company's top executives have extensive managerial experience on two or three continents. On the other hand, another company that prefers hiring local nationals for top countrywide responsibilities, sees itself as a large heterogeneous organization committed to cultural diversity and active citizenship in each of the foreign countries in which it does business.

By a wide majority both American and European companies prefer the latter course—the hiring of local nationals as top managers for local operations. Eighty percent of the U.S. companies in this survey said that the majority of company local or regional managers in foreign countries are local nationals, and for the European companies the figure is over 70 percent.

The reason why most companies are committed to this approach may well be that they think it makes good business sense. Roughly 85 percent of both the U.S. and European companies said that the presence of local nationals at the head of local operations was beneficial. In fact, a majority of those companies that do not have a local component headed by a foreigner said that local managers can be helpful. This compares with figures of under 30 percent of both U.S. and European companies that think foreigners at the board of directors and top management levels can advance their business prospects in foreign countries. Clearly, the likelihood of the practice of having foreigners at various different levels within the company is related to the perception of business advantage. While companies value the "insight" and "additional perspective" of foreigners at corporate levels, they do not see them as making a substantive contribution, as is the case with local nationals as managers of regional operations.

Indeed, for many companies, especially the American ones, the use of local nationals in top positions in their foreign branches goes to the essence of what it means to be an "international" organization. When asked what made their company "international," many of those interviewed said in effect: "Wherever we operate our local offices are headed by citizens of that country. It has always been company policy to hire local nationals, and that is what makes us an international company" (Exhibits 4 and 5).

There are qualifications to the widely shared preference for local nationals at the local level and they relate primarily to transfer of technology and the transfer of knowledge. An executive with a large European company, which has many high-technology products, explained why his organization often has difficulty in using foreign nationals at local levels:

"One of the characteristics of our company is the great interdependence between the different national organizations. This interdependence is necessary because products made in one country are sold in another country. I think that I am right in saying that we are not a company like Unilever that makes and sells products in one country. In our case it is more complicated. There are a few countries where this holds true for us, but only where it is enforced by government policy, as in the case of Brazil.

"These policies can cause us problems because most of our products are in fields which are hit by a high rate of inflation. We are under constant pressure to improve our technology and the means of delivering it. So from the brain center, which is mainly Western Europe, we have

RTZ's Philosophy

The development of the RTZ Group has been based on the acceptance of a true social responsibility towards employees, shareholders, customers and the communities where the Group companies operate. This is an evolutionary process which recognises the need to respond to changes in society and, perhaps more important, changes in the standards of acceptable behaviour by those whose livelihood is directly or indirectly affected. But there are, RTZ believes, certain fundamental assumptions which must be accepted. First and foremost is the recognition of the reasonable requirements and aspirations of the governments of the countries in which the Group companies operate. These include, particularly in the field of raw materials, the involvement of their own nationals in management at all levels; the participation of their nationals in the profit of the enterprise; and the assurance through the predominance on their boards, whether in executive or nonexecutive capacity, of nationals of their country, that its operations are not conducted in a manner which is contrary to the national interest.

This brings the further benefit that each member of the Group develops its own entrepreneurial attitudes and executes its own commercial policy, seeking to take advantage of opportunities which both expand its earning power and benefit the community in which it works. It is only in this way that there can emerge in the many companies separated by great distances and different cultures and environments a mutual respect for each other, and for the benefits to be derived from the willing interchange of technological and financial experience.

RTZ Explained, The Rio-Tinto Zinc Corporation Limited, 1981.

had to push new technologies out to other countries all the time. More and more, these local operations are dependent on this technology. This means that we have to have technical expertise out there all the time. Otherwise they will just be manufacturing out in Brazil without having the technical competence to absorb the new technology as it comes on. For this reason, we have to supplement these local operations with Dutchmen, Germans and Belgians.''

As the comment suggests, the distinction, particularly in a high-technology company, between the transfer of technology (how the product works) and the transfer of knowledge (how the company manufactures, sells and markets the product) is not always easy to make; but both are needed and both are often in short supply in foreign countries. In light of this difficulty, an American executive, whose company is active in both ''consumer driven'' and ''technology driven'' markets, preferred to concentrate on the availability of expertise in a given country: ''As between these two kinds of operations, I think it is often easier to find the local personnel in the high-technology area. After all, it is a matter of teaching

Characteristics of Unilever

Observed not only from the inside but from the outside too, it seems to be generally agreed that Unilever has a distinct style and personality of its own.

—We have a long history of working in different countries.

—Our companies are normally involved in national manufacture for national markets so there is close contact with consumers and the local society.

—We prefer employees to be nationals of their own countries, but it is our policy to have a small number of expatriate managers in each country in order to gain the benefits that come from different nationalities working together and to give managers international experience.

—We encourage contact between managers from different countries and, through international training, aim to foster an understanding and working style which enables Unilever managers to communicate easily with each other.

—We are scrupulous in our accounting and in our respect for the law.

—The Company only invests in activities with long term prospects, and which are in line with the general policies and aims of host countries.

The Responsibilities of Unilever, Unilever Limited, 1981.

one or two people the technology and you can find that small number in almost any country. With a consumer product you need a variety of skills; sales, marketing, and so on. You need depth for this kind of operation that is hard to get in some countries."

Evidently a company can find qualified local nationals if it is committed to doing so. Unilever notes its progress in this regard:

"In Sri Lanka in 1950 the management was 100 percent expatriate. Today it is 96 percent local (one expatriate, twenty-four nationals)."

"In Lever Brothers, Ghana, when the factory was first set up in 1961, expatriates constituted 63 percent of the management. Today they are 94 percent local (two expatriates, thirty nationals)."

"In Latin America, the proportion of expatriates in management has been halved since 1968 and is now only 10 percent (sixty-four expatriates, six hundred and fifty nationals)."[1]

Why Local Nationals—and Why Not

Assuming that qualified persons can be found, there is near unanimity of opinion as to the desirability of using local nationals to manage local operations[2] The reasons fall into three categories:

(1) *There is no choice: Local nationals are an absolute prerequisite for doing business in certain environments.* Executives cited two circumstances where this is the case. The first category is where the *host country* exerts strong pressure on the company to employ local nationals. A European executive described this situation: "In some countries, local managements are the prerequisite for doing business. For the most part these are developing nations, where board memberships are limited to local nationals or where work permits for foreigners are limited."

The other situation occurs when the subsidiary is an extremely large and important part of the parent company whose relative autonomy serves a *legal* as well as an *economic* purpose. A Swiss executive alluded to this situation:

"It may be that you have to manufacture locally in certain countries because some patent laws leave the

patent to expire or become void unless you work it. Then, of course, there are customs duties. The real reason, at the time, for Swiss and German companies starting local manufacturing particularly in the United States, was the prohibitive customs duties. In addition in the pharmaceutical area, for practical purposes, you have to do at least the compounding and the finishing in the United States even if you can import the product. The reason for this is the inspection issue. Otherwise, we would have to admit U.S. inspectors to inspect our premises."

In such situations, the company takes the risk of disturbing a delicate equilibrium that it has nurtured over the years were it to assign a home-country national to head a U.S. or Canadian subsidiary. The host-country government may become suspicious of a desire by the parent to exert more direct control, and local managers are concerned about potential threats to their prerogatives and independence of action.

Regardless of the reason a European company may have for establishing a local outpost in Canada or the United States, the markets they serve are sufficiently critical that some European executives have commented on the organizational necessity for elevating local managers in these countries to important positions. Of course, in the usual case, the company is not required by the host government, or pressured by its local subsidiary, to use local nationals. It simply makes good sense to use them because they are more likely to achieve good governmental relations and community support than are foreign nationals.

Although this rationale is cited by U.S. companies more often than by their European counterparts, it is considered important on both sides of the Atlantic. An American executive said: "In several countries where we have fully integrated operations (manufacturing and sales) it is essential to the functioning of the business that the senior executive have well-established channels of communication with the government and the business communities." Another U.S. executive observed that the involvement of local nationals "can minimize the risk of nationalization and the potential damage of hostile media focus." A third U.S. executive commented: "The degree to which the local community perceives that our operation is locally controlled affects the degree of receptivity and cooperation that we get from local business and banking."

For Europeans, the United States is one of the most important foreign countries. One European, whose company had merged with another large firm, recalled that the highly autonomous American subsidiary's knowledge and experience had been critical to the proposed merger:

"The American operations of both companies were so important and so large that if the consequence of the merger would have been that we would have to sell one

[1]Unilever and World Development, Unilever Limited, 1977.

[2]This has been the prevailing view for some time. See Michael G. Duerr and James Greene, *Foreign Nationals in International Management.* The Conference Board, Managing International Business, No. 2, 1968; and James R. Basche, Jr., *Integrating Foreign Subsidiaries into Host Countries.* The Conference Board, Report No. 506, 1970.

entire U.S. company, I don't think the merger would have gotten through. The fate of the merger hinged on the outcome of the U.S. negotiations.''

In addition, local managers within the United States are often considered essential for collective bargaining. A Swiss executive discussed the need for local handling of labor negotiations: ''Labor relations is one area where this need exists. We have a very firm philosophy that labor relations is the responsibility of the local people involved. In the case of the United States, our subsidiary keeps us informed so that we know if they are going to have a strike, but this has to be a local responsibility.''

(2) *Local nationals have a better understanding of the culture and environment in which the company is operating.* Both American and European companies acknowledge that an awareness of local culture, which local nationals possess, is critical to the proper conduct of business. On the whole, this demonstrates the emphasis observed in earlier case studies of having regional spokesmen who are familiar with the terrain.[3]

In these earlier investigations, Japanese, American and British executives all commented on the importance of having managers in various regions of their own countries who had lived in these cities and towns for many years, and who had close ties to the residents and an understanding of local problems. Indeed, although a U.S. executive is likely to say that it is important for a facility in Sao Paulo to be managed by a Brazilian who is familiar with that city, the individual would probably add that it is equally helpful for a factory in Omaha, Nebraska, to be headed by a long-standing resident of Omaha.

There is, however, a slight difference in emphasis. The Europeans see cultural sensitivity as important for achieving specific ends such as better governmental relations, a greater understanding of the needs of customers and markets, and good connections in the business and local communities. Americans view cultural sensitivity as more of an abstract concept and something to be valued in its own right. As one American put it: ''There can seldom be a substitute for the knowledge a foreigner has of his own country, its people, and their sensitivities. That sensitivity to the people often makes the difference between success and failure.''

This very general observation incorporates all of the more specific reasons for employing local nationals. But the frequency with which Americans express the view deserves special mention. When all the specific

rationalizations—such as the need for good governmental, customer and community relations, the importance of knowing the local labor market, and gaining access to sales channels—have been enumerated, there remains a single common denominator: A desire to be a good citizen of a foreign country and to blend harmoniously into the local environment.

As to more specific concerns, the knowledge of local markets is considered important. An American noted that ''local knowledge of markets and business styles assists in prompt execution,'' and another American executive commented: ''The use of local nationals to manage helps with local customers, gains more support, and provides local economic and cultural expertise.'' All of these relate back to the point raised by an executive with a large U.S. food company: ''In some countries, we sell soup under the same name with different ingredients in different parts of the country. In other countries, the peanut butter we sell in the south would be inedible to the people who buy our peanut butter in the north, and vice versa. You cannot expect someone in an office here in the United States to know these regional preferences in foreign countries.''

Many European managers agree with this formulation of the need for a local understanding of foreign markets. In fact, more Europeans considered this to be an important contribution for a local manager than did Americans.

(3) *Employing local nationals helps to achieve higher morale in local operations.*

Many U.S. companies argue that having local nationals in charge of foreign operations is essential to the maintenance of credibility with local nationals who are company employees at lower levels. These individuals also felt that local nationals in important managerial positions aided in the effective conduct of labor relations. When interviewed, European executives were quick to cite the autonomy and independence of their U.S. divisions, and the potential adverse effects on morale of giving top jobs to nationals from the company's home country.

A few companies, usually technology- or resource-driven firms, discount the importance of using local nationals. An executive from one such company explained: ''The foreign subsidiaries generally make and sell products comparable to those marketed in the United States. Top executive officers of the American corporate headquarters serve with locals on *foreign* boards for *each* subsidiary in each country. U.S. group vice presidents are responsible for comparable operations in the United States. American and foreign boards and executives are product-line oriented.''

For other high-technology companies, the issue is the demand for technical expertise in foreign environments.

---

[3]Allen R. Janger and Ronald E. Berenbeim, *External Challenges to Management Decisions: A Growing International Business Problem.* The Conference Board, Report No. 808, 1981.

One U.S. executive observed: "Our company's foreign offices are involved in exploration and production—specialized high-technology fields. With the exception of Canada and England, personnel with the required expertise are generally not available."

An executive with a large U.S. oil company observed that local governments and communities sometimes want heavy involvement from the parent company at the local level: "It is an issue of whether it is a high-technology operation, and how developed the country is. Where a lot of technical expertise is required and you have a less-developed country like Saudi Arabia, Iran or Venezuela, they *want* parent-company involvement. Where the job is less technical, or the country is more advanced, they care less about our direct involvement. Of course, these things are never explicitly stated. These countries just know that when they need this kind of help they will get it."

In the case of a large high-technology Dutch company, which has a great many "interdependent operations," mobility of the company's own nationals contributes to a decided preference for the use of home-country nationals in foreign locations. A spokesman for the company gave an explanation for his company's preference in this regard: "I think that we tend to have at least one Dutchman around in each of these foreign locations, if only to have very good contact with other countries. I do think that one of the reasons we have such a high percentage of Dutch people is the fact that we do not want local people to have certain positions for life. The trouble is that, in some countries, if you have somebody come into a position of top responsibility at the age of 40, the individual tends to stay there for 25 years. That is not in the interest of the company, but you cannot move such employees anywhere.

"On the other hand, Dutch people are more willing to move from one location to another. It is not our policy to have Dutch people there because they are Dutch, but because of their *mobility*. Also, these people grew up in headquarters. They know headquarters; many of them have moved from a small country to a bigger country or from a product division to a country headquarters, and in many countries that kind of experience is difficult to find. If you use local nationals, you can be stuck with someone for 25 years. If, after 10 years, you decide that you want to make a change, there may be no place that you can move the employee. If you fire the person, that will hurt the reputation of the firm—particularly if the individual is an influential local citizen. This is a very important principle within our organization."

Where They Use Them and Where They Don't

By a wide majority, the practices of U.S. and European companies reflect their stated preferences for hiring local nationals to run local operations wherever possible. In addition, the use of third-country nationals is also widespread in local outposts, but they are seldom in charge of a company's countrywide activities. Only one company, an American corporation, said that third-country nationals were the top managers in a majority of locations. This preference for local managers has been translated into practice; as already indicated, over 70 percent of the European companies employ local nationals as the heads of a majority of their foreign components, while the American figure is over 80 percent.

As to individual locations, companies are more likely to employ local or third-country nationals where the organization has a long history of commercial activity within the country, or where there is a well-established pattern of commercial relations between the home country and the region in which they want to do business. Thus, both American and European companies frequently have a local or third-country national at the helm of their U.S., British and West European operations. American firms, however, are more likely to have a local or third-country national in charge in Latin America than are Europeans. Both groups rely primarily on their own nationals in filling these positions in Asia, Africa and the Middle East (Table 8).

Although the practice of assigning local or third-country nationals to foreign positions is widespread, particularly in areas where the company has done business for a long time, there is little evidence that it is company policy, or *always* the case. Among both American and European companies, roughly 30 percent said that there were countries or regions where local operations are always headed by local nationals.

The small number of countries for which this is true, and the even smaller group of countries that are mentioned more than once, suggests that cultural sensitivities play a very small role in the decision not to choose company nationals for certain foreign posts. Still, these considerations are not entirely absent. A German executive was blunt in stating his company's policy with respect to France: "The company has always had a French manager in France. We cannot afford to delegate a German to France."

There are also concerns that are not directly related to local cultural issues. In this regard, one Venezuelan executive observed: "If a company sends someone out from headquarters whose major objective is a promotion, his emphasis will be on short-term returns. He gets that promotion and leaves a big mess behind. I have seen it happen."

By and large, U.S. and European companies feel that where local management is used, it is not necessary to use one of their own nationals as an observer, coordinator or for liaison purposes. Only one-sixth of both the American and European companies questioned reserve a

Table 8: Use of Local and Third-Country Nationals in Foreign Operations

Country or Region	Nationality of Parent Company			
	United States¹		Europe¹	
	Currently headed by local or third country national	Always headed by local²	Currently headed by local or third country national	Always headed by local²
United States...	—		14	7
Canada........	13	2	1	1
Western Europe				
Great Britain .	26	4	10	3
Austria......			2	
Belgium.....	6		1	1
Denmark.....			1	1
France......	15	8	11	4
Germany....	12	5	6	3
Italy........	5	2	3	1
Greece......	2			
Sweden.....	1	2	3	3
Norway......			2	
Netherlands..	3	2	3	
Portugal.....			1	
Spain.......	2	1	1	
Latin America				
Brazil.......	5	2	3	1
Mexico......	5	3		
Colombia....	1		1	
Argentina....	3	1		
Uruguay.....	1			
Venezuela...	2			
Australia......	11		2	1
New Zealand...	1			
Hong Kong.....	2			
India.........	1	2		
Japan.........	2	4		
North America..			1	
Europe........	2		1	
Latin America ..	1		1	
Pacific........	1			
Africa.........	2		1	
Mideast.......			1	
Number of Companies ..	85		44	

¹Details add to more than number of companies because of multiple responses.

²Denotes company policy which is not necessarily the current situation.

position other than the top spot for their own nationals, or prefer to have a national from the home country in charge of operations in certain locations.

With respect to those who always assign a home-country national to an important job in a foreign operation, no particular position emerges with any frequency. Four companies say that their policy is to assign their own nationals to the top financial job within local organizations. Another company selects one of its own nationals, or a third-country national, as either managing director or controller of a local operation. Finally, an American company, contrary to the usual practice, prefers its own nationals for the top labor or employee relations position in Great Britain, France, Belgium, Switzerland and Spain. A number of companies did not specify the position to which they assign their own nationals but said that they like to have at least one person in the leadership group of a local operation. In interviews, a number of executives commented that the objective of observation, coordination or liaison is often achieved by making top managers from the home-country members of the board of directors of local subsidiaries.

No clear pattern emerges as to which countries are singled out for leadership by expatriates from the home country. Many executives observed when interviewed that new operations regardless of country are usually headed by home-country personnel. While developing countries such as Ghana, Saudi Arabia, and the United Arab Emirates were cited in this regard, Australia, Great Britain, and the Netherlands were also mentioned.

The Ideal Expatriate

Although there is a widespread preference among both U.S. and European companies for hiring local nationals for important positions in foreign operations, it is often necessary to assign individuals from the home country to foreign locations. There is a good deal of agreement among both U.S. and European executives as to the right kind of person for this sort of job.[4] There are, nonetheless, some differences in emphasis.

Both American and European companies stress the fundamentals: management skill, product knowledge, and marketing know-how. Europeans are more likely than Americans to say that the requirements are no different than in the home country. One European drew an important distinction between the need for greater cultural sensitivity in certain areas than in others. This individual stressed the importance of "managerial competence and knowledge of the local way of life," and added that "the latter is of more importance in foreign countries outside Europe and the United States."

A U.S. oil company executive provided a checklist of criteria with which few respondents, American or European, would disagree:

"The management characteristics effective in the

---

[4]For more detail on this issue see Burton W. Teague, *Selecting and Orienting Staff for Services Overseas.* The Conference Board, Report No. 705, 1976.

United States are, and ought to be, essentially the same as employed abroad. Concern for corporate performance, knowledge of products and services, competence in employee relations, and knowledge of culture and traditions are paramount regardless of national borders.

"If there is one distinguishing characteristic, it is perhaps one of degree: The manager overseas must have a wider range of expertise. A solid background of managerial performance, a mastery of relevant technology, the broadest possible exposure to a variety of company operations, and a broad cultural and educational background are helpful.

"A successful manager must recognize the necessity of hearing and appreciating the viewpoints of the nationals with whom he deals. There must be give-and-take in sharing information and experiences. Managers must understand that the American way is not always 'right.'

"Other important characteristics for effective managerial performance in foreign countries include loyalty to the parent company and an understanding of the relationship of the local national interests to the corporate international interests; proficiency in the local language; ability to present parent-company views and positions to local governments, industry associations, and national employees; and the ability to translate corporate objectives into plans and programs that are in harmony with local social, economic, political and cultural standards. A college degree with liberal arts exposure is helpful. As the foreign manager is often alone, he must be decisive and a risk taker."

To this list of necessary attributes many of those interviewed would add one additional requirement: training skill. For many of the home-country nationals sent out by their corporate headquarters training a local national who can succeed them as the head of the local operation is one of the most important objectives of their tour of duty. In addition, these individuals often have the responsibility for staffing the local organization with qualified personnel at lower levels and many of these positions have important technical requirements. All in all, training and staffing experience is an important component of the expatriate manager's mix of skills. The chairman of a large Anglo-Dutch concern emphasized the importance of these attributes in discussing his firm's experience with various national groups as expatriates:

"The Australians are excellent expatriates, and we have used Australians in a large number of our overseas territories. They're very good training people. They fit in well. We have had Australians in important positions in our business in Malaysia, Brazil, Japan and in this country (Great Britain). They have taken Filipinos and Indonesians and given them jobs in their country and company. They provide a very good training ground for us which fits very well into our overseas pattern.

"South Africans are similar to Australians, although it is not as easy to transfer South Africans as Australians because there are many countries that you cannot send them to. You cannot send them to Nigeria or send Nigerians to South Africa. We do use them where we can: At the moment, the head of our business in Argentina is a South African and we have a Dutchman heading up the South African operation. So, even with South Africa, there is plenty of movement and transferability."

In the long run, home- and third-country nationals are used by most companies to establish an outpost in a foreign environment where the company's experience, skills and expertise are translated into the goods and services that the company then markets and sells. The primary medium for this process has always been, and always will be, people. The ideal expatriate's job is essentially one of *transmission* consistent with the company's objectives. In line with this view, the chief executive of one of the world's largest international companies observed: "The movement of people is *the* way to transfer technology. It is no good to send the handbook round and say, 'look, do it this way.' The way you do it is by sending around the people who can do it."

The Language Imperative

One test of a company's commitment to supplying expatriate managers with a sympathetic understanding of local cultures is its requirement with respect to the native language. Of course, in each instance there are two means of satisfying this demand: The company can employ a local national as its top executive or it can establish language facility as a prerequisite for the job in its selection of its own nationals, or third-country nationals, for the position.

The practices of U.S. and European companies in this regard are similar. A majority of both U.S. and European companies reported that their local managers in Europe and Latin America usually speak the local language. (See Table 9.)

Expatriate managers in other parts of the world are considerably less likely to speak the local language. In the Middle East, roughly half of the local operational heads for both American and European companies usually speak the language of the country. Among U.S. companies, more than half answered that their local manager usually speaks the native language in African and Asian countries. This figure was considerably lower among European firms.

While there are relatively few differences between U.S. and European organizations in practice, there is considerable difference in policy. A very large percentage of the European concerns *require* their local managers to speak the native language in other European countries and in Latin America. Only one-fifth of the U.S. companies have this prerequisite for European assign-

Table 9: Language Requirements for Local Managers
85 U.S. Companies

| | Ability to Speak Local Language | | |
Region	Company policy	Not policy— usually the case	Not Policy— infrequently the case
Latin America.	13	33	2
Europe.......	10	37	3
Middle East...	1	13	12
Africa........	1	14	12
Asia	3	18	16

44 European Companies

| | Ability to Speak Local Language | | |
Region	Company Policy	Not Policy— usually the case	Not Policy— infrequently the case
Latin America.	16	4	2
Europe.......	22	6	1
Middle East...	1	7	8
Africa........	3	4	10
Asia	1	5	11

ments and one-fourth have it for Latin America. In addition, 20 U.S. companies said that knowledge of the local language was not necessary at any location; only one European organization made that statement.

Finally, there is evidence that, regardless of the assignment or the nationality of the individual in question, a working knowledge of English is considered essential for a local manager of a European company. One respondent stated that "fluency in English at a minimum" was an important skill for such a position.

Incentives and Disincentives for Expatriates

The widespread utilization of local nationals for important positions is due in part to other conditions besides the need for sensitivity to local problems. It is becoming increasingly difficult to get qualified home-country nationals to accept foreign assignments. U.S. and European companies cite some common problems with respect to persuading promising executives to accept foreign assignments:

• Foreign positions are no longer as glamorous as they used to be. Increasingly, executives and their families value a comfortable and familiar life-style. In this regard, European countries, the United States, Canada, Australia and New Zealand are often considered more palatable than Asian, African or Latin American locations.

• Company loyalties and employee commitment are not the only factor in an employee's deliberation over whether to take a foreign post. Appeals that the organization vitally needs this service at the present time are likely to be weighed against competing family considerations. More often than has been true in the past, the company loses in this kind of equation.

• Ambitious and qualified managers are concerned about their careers after they return. They want more in the way of guarantees that a foreign assignment is part of a well-conceived career plan.

• The schooling of children is a critical consideration. Both U.S. and European executives say that the company has a strong bargaining point if it can promise to get a manager out and back before the children are in school.

• Managers want a foreign assignment to be of a finite duration. In the not too distant past, companies could send executives to a foreign country with a commitment that they would stay until a particular organizational objective was achieved. Increasingly, managers are asking that their assignments be limited to a specific number of years. This usually means that a qualified successor to the individual who is sent by the company will have to be found and trained fairly quickly.

• Those executives who do accept foreign assignments are more likely to drive a hard bargain with respect to authority, autonomy and the recruitment and deployment of those under their supervision in the new location.

In addition, U.S. companies are finding the "two career family" to be a barrier to getting an individual to accept a foreign assignment. For the most part, Europeans have not complained of this problem. Many added, however, that it is only a matter of time before it becomes an issue for them. In this regard, no organization, American or European, said that it makes an effort to find the spouse employment as part of the package that it negotiates with the employee.

All of these problems in making a foreign assignment boil down to a key point. The individual has become more important in the corporate scheme of things than has previously been the case, and companies are having to develop policies to accommodate needs and concerns of affected persons which have not been voiced in the past. These limitations inevitably lead to the employment of more local nationals. The chairman of a large

European corporation explained why this development, if properly understood and accepted, can work to the company's advantage:

"Fifteen to twenty years ago when managers went abroad, they went for an indefinite period. Sometimes they were expected to go for quite a long time. Now I think our average length of time will be in the area of five years. So, chaps may say, 'I do want to live in England and bring up my children in England, but I appreciate that five years in Indonesia will do my career a lot of good; I'm happy to take it on.'

"And those shorter assignments, in fact, suit us because of the desire and opportunity to promote local people. So you send a man out to Indonesia for five years as a chief accountant. He has an important job to do in running that department efficiently, and he also has to train his successor. The Indonesians, who are good accountants, won't want to see him hanging on there for too long. So it is a healthy move all the way around."

Sometimes the problem for a company is not getting someone to go to a location, but in persuading the person to return. This difficulty is more often a problem for European firms. One executive described how his company responds to these situations:

"Sometimes the man will want to stay. If it suits us for him to stay there and it suits everybody, we would, of course, try to accede to his wishes. But if it does not suit us, we will not allow it.

"There are a few places where this arises most often. North America is one of them. You send someone to Canada and he finds a comfortable life, with a salary twice what he would get here, and he wants to stay. Another place where we sometimes find people wanting to stay is Australia.

"These people say, 'I prefer not to take that job back home. My children are getting on well in school here. I like what I am doing and there is no one to succeed me. I would be happy to stay. Give me another term.' We say

OK, but you are taking a bigger risk because that opening may not be there the next time around."

There are a group of individuals who, in the experience of one company, are quite happy to get foreign assignments, and quite willing to leave them when their tour of duty has been completed: third-country nationals from developing countries. A European chief executive gave some of the reasons for their flexibility in this regard:

"There is also the phenomenon of moving people from developing countries to other developing countries, and that is increasingly attractive to some people.

"One of the reasons for this attraction is that they come from communities that sometimes have a rather narrow range of opportunities. Financially, of course, it can be very beneficial for people from countries like India, where there are grave salary and tax limitations. Very often the only way an Indian manager can put aside a little bit of money is by being lucky enough to be posted to Saudi Arabia."

* * *

In sum, American and European companies agree that it is getting harder to recruit qualified home-country nationals for service in foreign countries. Moreover, the recruitment process requires more in the way of negotiation of terms for the individual foreign assignment, and a commitment that the person in question will receive a good position upon returning. Despite this greater difficulty, those interviewed expressed satisfaction that the individuals who did accept these offers were of as high a caliber, or higher in some cases, than those whom the company had sent to foreign posts in the past. Many agree that only top people were even considered for such positions and that experience of this nature is indispensable for the ambitious manager.

Chapter 4
Internationalism: Supporting Administrative Systems

CLEARLY, achieving an international outlook depends on the selection and use of people at various levels within the organization. However, companies also rely on procedures and communications to achieve an international perspective.

• *Procedures:* There is a necessary distinction between formal and informal procedures. Formal procedures exist for two major purposes: planning and auditing. Most organizations hold large planning sessions that involve regional or country managers from all over the world.[1] This process facilitates a multilateral exchange of views in that managers from various locations have an opportunity to discuss matters of mutual concern with headquarters. Patterns and trends can be observed. Headquarters can get information out to a large number of subsidiaries and regional managers can make their views known to company leadership. Managers from different parts of the world can exchange problems and solutions.

In contrast, the auditing process is bilateral in nature. It is an opportunity for a one-on-one discussion. Both auditing and planning are considered indispensable in developing understanding of world and local conditions. In addition, these processes facilitate the integration of this information into the company's overall plans and the formulation of coherent objectives that enable the organization to speak with one voice at both the corporate and the local level.

Notwithstanding their important role for an international company, planning and auditing, as a German planning director noted, play a similar part in domestic operations. Planning and audit procedures were not developed as a response to the need for greater in-

ternational understanding and there is little evidence that these procedures differ markedly between the international and the domestic spheres.

• *Informal communications:* Informal communications are specifically tailored to a company's individual international requirements. Among the variety of methods used are informal regional meetings and opportunities for the regional manager to go to company headquarters to discuss specific problems.

In addition, many companies emphasize employee communications. Most often cited as an example of informal employee communication is the organization's magazine. (In some instances there may be more than one.) These publications are often highly professional in appearance and contents and they help to call attention to the diversity of the company's operations and interests. If that were all these house organs accomplished, the same purpose might be achieved by the annual report. The additional dimension provided by these magazines is that they help to develop the awareness and *esprit de corps* of employees as members of a truly global organization. The journal can also serve as a clearing house for practical advice on what to do if, for example, one is transferred to Brazil, or how to handle the problems associated with return.

Employee publications also help to achieve a level of standardization and uniformity in written communications. Many are published in English and go out to local managers all over the world. The existence of a common language in which employees can communicate, as well as publications which serve as a conduit for this communication, gives international business organizations an ease and facility in communications that other multinational organizations do not share. These other organizations are, of course, hampered by political considerations. There are no such barriers to standardization in an international business. The company can simply state that the language of the company will be English for major transactions and, in the process,

---

[1] For a recent look at the international aspects of planning see James R. Basche, Jr., *International Dimensions of Planning.* The Conference Board, Research Bulletin No. 102, 1981.

dismantle one of the major barriers to the free and easy exchange of views over national boundaries.

In addition to publications, many companies have training courses and international briefings, which are requirements for regional managers. These meetings promote contact between local managers and offer an opportunity for them to discuss their problems with key company executives.

The Centralization-Decentralization Issue

However committed a company may be to internationalism and the discrete local identity of its foreign operations, organizations want certain areas to remain highly centralized. These functions include:

• *Finance:* Every company interviewed imposes limitations on capital expenditures by local subsidiaries, regardless of the degree of autonomy which the subsidiary may possess by virtue of local law or company practice. These amounts may vary within a given company according to the subsidiary's size, length of time in operation, or country, but the subsidiaries of the major companies interviewed for this study all operate under some sort of capital-expenditure restriction. In addition, all local operations or subsidiaries must obtain approval for the means by which they obtain the money they propose to spend—borrowings, public offerings, and so on.

The need for uniformity in the reporting and valuing of assets and earnings insures that financial operations will remain a centralized function for the foreseeable future, and that one of the primary centralizing thrusts of the international corporation will be its financial management.

• *Personnel:* Companies regard the demand for local financial participation and the explicit or implicit insistence by local governments that the company hire local nationals as a challenge to their centralized personnel administration for higher level positions in local operations. For many organizations centralized record keeping is all that remains of a once centralized personnel system for top executives in foreign offices. Other firms report that they still have a strong centralized personnel function to monitor the management development system. While a company may be able to report satisfaction with its personnel process on a worldwide basis, the integration of a particular operation into a global design may be a problem.

• *Research:* Research is also an area where companies are fighting hard to preserve a centralized approach. Moreover, the same tendency—a demand for local participation in the name of nationalism—is challenging that position. Centralized research is preferred by many companies for three reasons: (1) greater economy; (2)

better coordination between research and its two major objectives: improving existing products and developing new ones, and (3) the need to protect the integrity of product designs and specifications. Arguing the first two points, the Chief Executive of a large Anglo-Dutch firm said:

"I still feel it is correct for us to concentrate our central research effort in Europe. The three laboratories form a central group where many scientific disciplines are available to the whole concern and through which we maintain a clear 'window' on the scientific world. Thus, central research has generated a huge data bank of technical information, which is available to our companies throughout the world. This may well be the most valuable single contribution that research makes to the growing technical strength of our overseas companies."

The problem is, as this individual readily concedes, that local governments do not always agree. The demand that technology be allowed to "grow" once it takes root in the soil of a country is, increasingly, being articulated by developing countries.

In addition, some of the local governments are arguing that a company cannot charge its local operation in that particular country a service fee for the use of its research technology. There are reports of service fees being refused or limited in Brazil, Turkey and India. The objective of this prohibition is to require the company to do its research locally. This creates problems for the local company in developing its technology, and difficulties for the parent in meeting its research costs. As this individual continued:

"In some cases, for instance, we are providing the rent of our technology and in other instances a very wide range of services. I mean the whole of our research, the whole of our head office, the things we provide at the center to help companies run smoothly. They have to be paid for in some way, and just to pay for them with the dividend on 40 percent of the shareholding is not enough. All that does is remunerate our capital, but it does not pay the other services which are involved."

A collateral concern raised by the demand for more local participation in research is that the necessary uniformity in technical specifications may not be preserved. At this time, large international corporations are active in relatively few industries. Many of these businesses—electronics, chemicals, drugs and farm machinery, to name some of the more prominent examples—require a high degree of uniformity in product specification, ingredients or design. For this reason, and because of the importance of protecting the reputation of the trademark (particularly in the drug and chemical fields), this aspect of company operations will remain resistent to the demand for local participation and control.